BIBLICAL EXEGESIS

A Beginner's Handbook

Second Edition

John H. Hayes and Carl R. Holladay

SCM PRESS LTD

220.6

334 00123 4

First published 1982 by John Knox Press, Atlanta
First British edition published 1983
by SCM Press Ltd
26-30 Tottenham Road, London N1
Second edition 1988

Printed in the United States of America

Contents

CHAPTER 1

Introducing EXEGESIS

Exegesis as an Everyday Activity and as a Specialized Discipline

Exegesis is a normal activity in which all of us engage every day of our lives. Whenever we hear an oral statement or read a written one and seek to understand what has been said, we are engaging in exegesis.

The term "exegesis" itself comes from the Greek word *exegeomai* which basically meant "to lead out of." When applied to texts, it denoted the "reading out" of the meaning. The noun, therefore, could refer to "interpretation" or "explanation." Thus whenever we read a text or hear a statement which we seek to understand and interpret, we are involved in exegesis.

Although we do not today label our interpretation of oral and written words as "exegesis," this is nonetheless the activity in which we engage. Only when there is exegesis is there communication and understanding. When one person speaks to another person, the hearer must decide what is said and what is meant. Automatically, the hearer asks certain questions about what was said. Was it a question or a statement? Is the speaker seeking to communicate something? If so, what? Are the words spoken to be taken literally or are they conventional or symbolic statements or greetings? Am I, as the hearer, expected to respond? What thoughts is the speaker trying to convey? What form are the words spoken in? Is the speaker telling a joke? reporting some news? addressing a demand? asking for information? giving a lecture? trying to sell a product? As persons accustomed to speaking and listening, we can usually go through the process of exegesis without much effort, in fact, almost unconscious of the process itself.

Since such oral communication generally takes place in familiar situations and with familiar persons, we are able to assess the context and intentions of the speaker as well as to analyze the spoken words themselves. The context helps us to determine the larger complex in which the event of communication takes place and thus to understand the words spoken. Is it a superior and/or an official who is giving commands, offering directions, supplying information, or making suggestions? Is it a formal and/or structured situation in which the spoken words are to be taken seriously or merely a casual situation? Is it conversation between friends? Were the words spoken under normal or abnormal conditions? Part of the process of understanding oral communication, therefore, involves the context and occasion in which speech takes place. This means that the speaker, the words, the context, and the listener all participate in the communication process.

A similar but not identical situation takes place when we read texts or written words. Since the writer is generally not present when we read a text or a document, the words themselves assume a greater importance than in a situation of oral communication. It is true that readers can frequently, through imagination and prior knowledge, re-create in their minds something of the writer and the situation in which the text was written, when this is necessary. For exmple, if we receive letters from friends, we have some knowledge about the persons and their situations which informs our reading of the written words. Nevertheless, even in reading a letter from a friend or member of our family, we engage in exegesis. We seek to understand what is said and what it means. We interpret the words so as to understand what is being communicated.

Every day we interpret written texts with little or only very general knowledge about the writer. Here, communication takes place primarily between the text and the reader, and the writer, unlike the speaker in oral communication, becomes less important. It is true, of course, that the writer and the reader usually share a common world, common frames of reference, and a common understanding and use of language. To this extent, the writer and the reader are not very remote from one another. When one, for example, reads a highway sign or a traffic direction, it matters little who the writer of the words happens to be. All that is required is that the reader and the text on the sign share in a common linguistic field of reference. The written directions on the sign or the symbols used need only make sense to the reader and lend themselves to exegetical understanding. Even highway signs illustrate not only the necessity for exegesis but also the difficulties sometimes involved. For example, does a highway sign that reads "Road Construction 1500 Feet" mean that for the next 1500 feet a driver should expect construction activity or that after traveling 1500 feet a driver should expect to encounter construction activity? Such a message demands special exegesis and, in this case, the exegesis probably requires prior experience in understanding such signs.

We constantly read and exegete multiple forms of written texts. The average student in a day may read an assignment in a scientific textbook, a short story, a poem, labels on food containers, announcements of meetings and other events, a newspaper, a letter, an advertising brochure, the telephone directory, and on and on. All of these texts assume different forms of communication and represent different types or genres of written documents. Since these texts are all part of our normal culture, we have been socialized and acculturated into how to read and understand them in all their diversity. We know that one does not read and interpret a poem in the same way as a recipe nor the editorial page in the same manner as the front page of a newspaper.

Even in our culture, there are types of documents and literature which require special and intensive exegetical work. In fact, there are professions which specialize in the exegesis and interpretation of texts. The need for these arises from the nature of certain texts and their use of specialized and technical contents and terminology. Legal and judicial professions—lawyers and judges—spend much of their time exegeting laws and law codes and studying the history of their interpretation and application. Constitutional lawyers specialize in the exegesis of the constitution and the history of its interpretation. Diplomatic language and documents often require a special exegesis since communication in this area is frequently very sensitive and deliberately ambiguous.

The required effort and means necessary for the exegesis and interpretation of texts thus vary greatly, depending upon the nature of the texts and their relationship to normal communication. Some texts merely need to be read to be understood. Others require very detailed analysis. Some use normal, everyday language, grammar, and sentence structure. Others use a very specialized vocabulary, involved grammatical and sentence structure, and distinctive forms of expression. Some texts employ symbolic and metaphoric language. Others seek to employ language and words so as to limit severely the range of meaning and the potential for multiple interpretations and misunderstanding. Some texts seek to persuade. Others seek merely to inform. Some texts are produced to entertain. Others seek to produce some particular response and action.

The degree of difficulty involved in exegeting and interpreting a wide range of texts, and oral communication as well, depends upon two basic variables. (a) A primary factor involves the degree to which the sender (the speaker, author, or editor/collector) and the receiver (the hearer or reader) share a common world of discourse and experience. When two persons who share a common language talk or write to one another, very few problems of communication develop. Few difficulties are to be expected when they exegete and interpret one another's oral and written statements. The greater the difference between their normal fields of discourse and the greater the disparity between their range of experience, the greater will be the difficulty of their communication. They will experience greater difficulty in exegeting and interpreting each other's forms of communication and what is being communicated. For example, two persons from a similar rural environment or two persons from a similar urban environment would probably have little difficulty in communicating with each other whether in written or oral form. The situation, however, might be very different when the city dweller and the rural person seek to communicate.

(b) A further factor involves the extent to which the communication and the form in which it occurs involves specialized content and forms of expression. This point can be illustrated by using examples drawn from letter writing. Personal letters, one of the most common means of personal communication, are generally written in a straightforward manner and vary in content and form depending upon the degree of familiarity existing between the senders and receivers and the content to be communicated. As we all know, however, various types of letters require different approaches to interpretation and exegesis. Most letters—say from a friend or a parent—require little effort in understanding. A specialized letter—say from a technician describing some mechanical or chemical process or from an accountant explaining a bookkeeping procedure—is a totally different matter. In a similar fashion, an essay on Paris in the springtime would probably present fewer interpretive problems than an essay on the influence of Renaissance architecture on nineteenth-century constructions in Paris.

Complexity is introduced into the exegetical process by a number of factors. (1) The first of these is what can be called the "third-party perspective." Often in seeking to understand texts, the interpreter is not one of the primary or original parties in the communication event. In this case, the interpreter is neither the sender nor the receiver but a third party who is, in a sense, an outsider, an observer, or even an intruder. Letters, for example, are much more difficult to interpret when being read by a third party. In such a situation, the parties to the original communication may be totally unknown to the interpreter. Generally most documents are best understood when the sender has some prior knowledge of the receiver and the receiver has some prior acquaintance with the sender. This makes it possible for the sender to hypothesize how the communication will be received and understood and thus shape and express the communication accordingly. The receiver in like fashion can hypothesize about the sender so as to understand better both the content and the shape of the communication. The third party must seek to understand the communication by assuming the role of or by empathizing with both the sender and the receiver. The interpreter must try to read the document 'as if'' the interpreter were both the sender and the receiver. This requires the interpreter—the third party—to search out information about both the sender and the receiver and their situations. When the content or form of the document is very specialized, unique, or ambiguous, this process is required to an even greater degree.

(2) A second complexity is introduced when the text or document is composed in a language different from that of the interpreter or exegete. Here a language barrier intrudes into the interpretive or exegetical process. If an English speaking person wants to read a German language textbook or receives a letter from a German, for example, the reader or interpreter is confronted with special problems. The English interpreter must either acquire sufficient knowledge of German to read the text or resort to a translator who can aid in overcoming the language barrier. Since each language has its own distinctive structure, grammatical features, and vocabulary nuances, it is very difficult for an outsider to acquire the proficiency of the native. When translations are made they are themselves already interpretations, since it is never possible for a translation to be an exact one-to-one transference from one language to another. An interpretation of a translation is what might be called a ''second-level interpretation.''A first-level interpretation is the interpretation made of the original, whether by a native speaker or hearer or by one who has acquired knowledge of the original language. What appears in a translation is the translator's understanding of the original. The second level of interpretation enters the picture when an interpreter seeks to understand the content of the translation. Although translations help to bridge the gap between one language and another, they can never do so completely.

(3) A third factor which frequently must be taken into consideration in the exegesis of texts is what might be called the ''cultural gap.'' Documents produced in one cultural context and exegeted in another cultural

context present certain problems to the interpreter. There are two reasons for this. First of all, such a document may explicitly mention, describe, or allude to special ideas, practices, and customs which would be clearly understood by a person reading the document in the original culture but which baffle a reader in a different culture. In the second place, communication within a culture frequently assumes a shared body of cultural understanding. This general reservoir of experience, worldview, and perception which lies behind the text would not be shared by the cultural outsider. A document, for example, reporting the actions and outcome of a particular sporting event, say a baseball game or a cricket match, would present difficulties in interpretation for a person living in a culture where the sport and its rules of play were unknown phenomena. This difference in cultures is not just related to ideas, concepts, and worldviews. Also involved are differences in the way things are said and written and the customary way of reading and interpreting. In some cultures, for example, when one tells a story, the first character to be mentioned is always the villain. Generally, the more remote and different the culture presupposed and reflected in the document from that of the interpreter, the greater the difficulty the exegete encounters in interpreting the text.

(4) A fourth factor which can introduce perplexity in exegeting texts is what can be called "the historical gap." A person in the present studying a document from the past is separated chronologically from the time when the document was produced. The gap between the past and the present does not have to be great in order to see this factor in operation and to experience some of its consequences.

Reading a newspaper that is, let us say, fifty years old, can be a fascinating and question-raising experience. One notices, for example, differences from the present in clothing fashions, in prices for advertised items, in issues that were the concerns of the day, in the manner in which articles were written, and on and on. Questions arise immediately. Why were things that way? Why were certain issues and events considered important? How could prices be so low? How could people have thought and reacted the way they did? When we read documents from the more distant past—say from the days of ancient Greece and Rome—we often encounter matters that are a "world apart" from the present—persons and places, practices and perspectives, customs and conventions, and so on. This is why editions of the ancient classics are often provided with notes to explain historical facts and features that are anchored in the past and no longer a part of the living present.

(5) A fifth factor that can complicate the exegetical process is the fact that documents are sometimes the products of collective and historical growth. This means that documents are, on occasion, not the product of a single author nor even of one particular period of time. The United States constitution, for example, was produced by a constitutional convention and many figures contributed to its formation. In addition, the original document has been added to in the form of amendments. We are all familiar with different editions of textbooks. Often a textbook, written by one author, will be revised by a second author so that it may no longer be possible to distinguish original material from added material unless we have access to the various editions. College and university catalogues are representative of literature that has come into being through growth and collective contributions. Much information in a current catalogue may have been there since the first catalogue published by the school. Other items may be the results of recent policy decisions. If a researcher wished to explore the development of the school's policies and curriculum but possessed only the current catalogue, it would be a formidable if not an impossible feat! By comparison of the catalogue with information gained from other sources, it might be possible to deduce some conclusions. For example, one could hypothesize when courses in nuclear physics or liberation theology were introduced or when coeducational dormitories became permissible.

In the ancient world, there was a far greater tendency for works to be the product of collective growth than is currently the case. Even in medieval times, writers often sought *not* to be original. Instead they frequently edited and combined older works which, sometimes, were themselves already edited and augmented works. This means that ancient works were frequently the products of a long and complex editorial process and contained layers or strata of materials and traditions. The ancient Jewish historian, Josephus, for example, utilized assistants in his writing, so that some of his works were really the product of a joint effort. In addition, he frequently incorporated or rewrote sources without acknowledging that he was actually doing this or informing the reader about the sources being used. In defense of Josephus and many of his ancient counterparts, however, it must be noted that this was fairly common practice in those times before the rise of the modern interest in authors and authorship and the development of copyright laws. The results of this process of growth and historical development can occasionally be seen in "seams" in the material, anachronisms in the text, differences in style, and even contradictions in the contents. In the exegetical study of such documents, this character of the texts must be taken into consideration.

One further consideration should be noted at this point about literary productions in antiquity. Works were sometimes produced as if they were the work of someone else, generally some venerable figure from the past. A writer, at a later point in time, would produce a work and attribute it to a person of the remote or recent past. Occasionally such writers probably felt they were expressing what would have been the thoughts of the one under whose name they wrote, maybe even preserving some authentic material. Sometimes such works were produced by students or followers of important figures in order to pass on their teacher's or leader's legacy. Works produced this way tended to be associated with and attributed to the revered personality rather than to the students or the followers since such works could embody the former's thought and the latter were generally less well-known. An example of this would be the numerous philosophical treatises attributed to Aristotle, now known to be spurious and written many years after his death. Occasionally persons followed this practice to give their works an authoritative appeal. An example of this phenomenon can be seen in the enormous amount of literature that was written under the name of Enoch to whom the Bible gives only incidental notice (see Genesis 4:17–18; 5:18–24). None of these Enochian writings made their way into the Scriptures although they are referred to in Jude 14–15. Generally the nature of such works, called pseudepigraphs, can be discovered by analyzing the texts from literary, linguistic, and historical perspectives.

(6) A sixth factor which can contribute to complexity and difficulty in the exegetical process is the existence of multiple and differing texts of the same documents. Frequently two or more copies of a given document exist but with lesser or greater differences between the copies. At this point, the interpreter is confronted with the problem of determining the actual wording of the text to be interpreted. Differences between copies of the same work are much more common for ancient than for modern works. The issue of divergent texts of the same work, however, is not unknown even after the use of the printing press became widespread in the fifteenth and sixteenth centuries. For example, many of the plays of Shakespeare exist in significantly differing texts, so much so, that the study of texts of Shakespeare's plays has been a highly developed and controversial field. Before the use of the printing press, copies of texts were always made by hand. Handcopying of any text of any length generally results in varying numbers of mistakes—such as mis-

spellings, omitted words or units, repeated words or units, and so forth. We possess few texts from antiquity in their original form, the so-called autographs. Most often what we have are actually copies of copies of the original. Since no one copy of any text of major size agrees exactly with another copy of the same text, this requires the exegete to confront the problem of the text in its original or authorial form.

The problem of multiple and differing texts of the same work can become more complicated when differences between texts are also represented in several languages. If differences between various copies exist but all the copies are in the same language, this presents the problem in one dimension. If there are diverging copies of the same work in several languages, this adds another dimension. Copies of manuscripts of Aristole's works, for example, exist in Greek, Latin, and Arabic. Where there are significant differences between these, the exegete must work across language boundaries in order to try and discover what appears to be the most likely reading.

(7) A seventh and final factor to be considered in noting the complexities that can develop in exegesis is the fact that some texts are considered sacred and thus different in some fashion from all other works. To treat a text as sacred in some sense involves more than treating it as good literature or as a classical work.

We are all familiar with the concept of the classical works of Western literature reflected in introductory English literature anthologies. There are certain well-accepted criteria by which literary works are recognized as "classics." Among these are the following: (a) a work must be well-written and a good example of its genre; (b) it must engage isssues and concerns that are reflective of recurring human conditions; and (c) it must possess a quality which lends itself to multiple if not infinite interpretability, that is, it must be open to diverse readings and understandings.

A sacred text may possess some or all of the characteristics of a classic. Other dimensions enter the picture, however, when the work falls into the category of the sacred. About classical works, people hold opinions; about sacred texts, they hold convictions. Sacred texts belong to the category of Scripture. There are several characteristics of "Scripture." (a) Scripture possesses an authority for someone or some group that exceeds normal conditions. This is true whether one is speaking metaphorically about the fisher's or hunter's or stamp collector's "bible" or realistically about the Moslem Koran or the Jewish and Christian Bibles. (b) As authoritative documents, Scriptures occupy an official position in the life of the communities or groups that regard them as Scripture. They are sources to which appeal is made and whose contents inform in a special way the lives of certain communities and their members. (c) Scriptures are understood as embodying a truer or better reflection and understanding of reality than is the case with other writings. (d) Reality itself or the voice, thought, or word of God is believed to be related to Scriptures in a way that is not true of other writings.

By their very nature, Scriptures bear special relationships to the communities that consider them sacred. The communities have frequently participated in their formation. Their sacredness is based on the fact that communities have chosen to assign them a special place and a special role. In addition, the manner in which the communities have understood and interpreted their Scriptures becomes a decisive influence in how they are assessed. Around Scriptures, there also develop assumptions and systems of thought that are often taken for granted as being both the result of the Scriptures' interpretation and as the standard by which they are to be interpreted or the lens through which they should be read. Around Scriptures, there develops a tradition of both what the texts say and how they are to be read. One who would exegete a sacred text thus stands in some fashion within a tradition with a long history in which the texts have interacted with the tradition and the tradition with the texts.

In this section, we have noted that exegesis is an activity in which all people engage when they interpret oral and written texts. Secondly, we noted that some conditions and texts require special efforts at interpretation and that exegesis can be a special discipline. Thirdly, we noted some factors that can complicate the exegetical process and make necessary certain special operations, special training, and special tools.

The Bible and Exegesis

Biblical exegesis belongs to the category of specialized exegesis. Reading and understanding the Bible are undertakings different in degree from reading and understanding a letter from a friend, an article in a contemporary magazine, a newspaper account of some event, or a modern novel or short story. The various complexities which can influence the exegetical process noted in the previous section are all related in one way or another to biblical exegesis. Let us note how all seven of these factors enter the picture in biblical exegesis.

(1) None of the Bible was originally addressed to the modern reader and interpreter. None of us was involved in the original communication

events as either senders or receivers. Paul's letters, for example, were written to the Romans, the Galatians, the Corinthians, and others. The modern interpreter, in the case of Paul, is therefore reading somebody else's mail. The books of Luke and Acts were accounts written for someone named Theophilus. These illustrations make clear that as students interpreting biblical materials we are, in a sense, third-party intruders and suffer from third-party perspectives.

(2) None of the Bible was originally composed in a modern language. The Old Testament was written in Hebrew and Aramaic and the New Testament in Greek. Even the modern Israeli who speaks Hebrew or the modern Greek who speaks Greek recognizes that the languages of the Bible are not the same as modern Hebrew and Greek. Thus all modern exegetes, in interpreting the Bible, encounter the problem of a language barrier.

(3) The modern readers of the Bible and the original readers of the texts are separated by an enormous cultural gap. The culture presupposed by the Bible is that of the ancient Mediterranean world in general and Palestine in particular. One has only to note a few general characteristics of biblical culture to sense its difference from much modern culture. The social structures presupposed by the writers of biblical materials were patriarchal and authoritarian. The dominant economic system was agriculturally and village based. Diets were seasonal. Medical arts were primitive. Machines were little developed. Slavery was widespread. General mortality, and especially infant mortality, rates were high. Travel was slow and difficult. Life was rather simple and characterized by stability and similarity rather than change. Human life was oriented to the cycles of nature and climate. Entertainment was limited. Good artificial lighting did not exist. Animals were slaughtered, dressed, and burned on altars as an integral part of worship. Divine beings, both good and bad, were assumed to be participants in the ongoing course of life and history.

(4) The historical gap that separates the present from the world of the Bible ranges from almost twenty centuries to over three millennia. The biblical traditions came into being during a period extending over twelve centuries. These factors suggest two reasons why the exegete must bridge this historical gap. First of all, the Bible originated within a context chronologically far removed from the present. Secondly, since the materials originated over such a long period of time, it becomes necessary to understand the different historical contexts within which the various books and traditions of the Bible came into being. In addition to

these two considerations, there are two factors internal to the Bible itself which demand historical attention on the part of the exegete. First, much of the Bible takes the form of historical narrative. To call the Bible a history book is a misleading simplifcation but it does point to the fact that much of the material is concerned with historical matters. This phenomenon cannot be ignored if one is to understand the Bible. Secondly, much of the thought and theology of the Bible is expressed in terms of past, present, and future, that is, in terms of a theology which both takes seriously the course of historical events and is expressed in categories dependent upon historical perspectives.

(5) The gradual growth of traditions and collective contributions to documents are clearly evident in the Bible, especially the Old Testament. In fact, it is impossible to speak of particular authors of documents in the Old Testament since we do not know who wrote a single book. Instead, most of the works appear to have developed over lesser and greater lengths of time and many persons probably contributed to their formation. If we take Amos as a typical example of a prophetical book, we can see the diversity of material in the book which makes it impossible to speak of Amos as the author. In the book, we find four types of material. (a) A superscription provides some historical data about the prophet (1:1). (b) Much of the book consists of oracles or speeches attributed to the prophet (1:2—6:14; 8:4–14; 9:5–15). (c) Some material is biographical, like the superscription, and speaks of the prophet in the third person (7:10–17). (d) Other material reports visions by the prophet and appears to be autobiographical with the prophet referring to himself in the first person (7:1–9; 8:1–3; 9:1–4). This diversity in the book suggests that it was clearly an edited work produced by someone other than the prophet himself. Practically all of the prophetic books manifest this same type of diversity.

Another way of looking at the books as the product of collective growth and authorship, in addition to the diversity in types of literary material, is to note changes in content and perspective or differences in historical conditions presupposed. Since the Middle Ages, scholars have noted that the historical conditions, the style of the speeches, and the content of Isaiah 1—39 differ from Isaiah 40—66. The former presupposes a struggling state of Judah defending itself against the aggressive and powerful Assyrian empire. The latter assumes that the Judeans are in exile and that a faltering Babylonian empire is the major political power. The former thus presupposes the historical conditions of the eighth century B.C. and the latter those of the sixth century B.C. To exegete and

interpret the latter half of Isaiah as if it came from the eighth century
would be like interpreting a contemporary document as if it came from
the eighteenth century. The book of Isaiah, therefore, like many portions
of the Old Testament, must be viewed as an anthology of materials coming from different periods.

(6) As with most documents from antiquity, the oldest manuscripts of
the Old and New Testaments we possess are copies made long after the
original documents were written. The oldest complete manuscript of the
Hebrew Bible dates from the Middle Ages (the copy was made in A.D.
1008). The oldest complete manuscript of the New Testament dates
from the fourth century A.D. About 5,000 different Greek manuscripts
or fragments of the New Testament are known. Of these, no two are
identical. The manuscript copies of the Hebrew Bible or parts thereof are
less numerous. In recent years, however, older fragments and almost
complete manuscripts of some books of the Old Testament have been
discovered in caves and other places in the Dead Sea region of Palestine.
Some of these show considerable differences from the standard Hebrew
texts.

Since the Bible was translated into other languages—such as Syriac,
Latin, and Coptic—quite early, these early versions also enter the picture in any attempt to determine the text of a passage or book. This is
particularly the case with the Old Testament which was translated into
Greek and Aramaic during the last centuries B.C. and the early centuries
A.D. In addition, the first five books of the Old Testament (the Pentateuch) also exist in an early Hebrew form known as Samaritan which differs frequently from the standard Hebrew text. All of this means, of
course, that textual studies in one form or another are indispensable in
biblical exegesis.

(7) That the Bible falls into the category of sacred Scripture needs no
special comment. Two matters, one positive and one negative, should be
noted. Positively, today's biblical exegete has been preceded by centuries of biblical study and interpretation which can be drawn upon for perspectives and insights. Negatively, the Bible as sacred Scripture has
been surrounded by tradition and traditional interpretations of various
sorts. The exegete is frequently tempted to read the text in light of the
tradition without any critical judgment or without letting the text speak
afresh and on its own. To do this is to engage in *eisegesis*, a "reading
into," rather than *exegesis*, a "reading out of."

The above considerations might seem to suggest that exegesis of the
Bible is a formidable if not impossible task. This might be the case if the

Bible in its manuscript and translated forms were a newly discovered ancient document and one had to approach its interpretation *de novo*— that is, learn all the languages, prepare the tools, and do all the necessary research. The biblical exegete, however, does not have to do this. Thousands of others throughout the centuries have interpreted the Bible, prepared tools available to the contemporary interpreter, and developed methods of approaching the problems and issues involved. Probably no other book has been so studied as the Bible, and tools for such study have been prepared by scholars who have spent their lives engaged in biblical exegesis and interpretation.

Biblical Exegesis Through the Centuries

From their earliest days, the synagogue and the church have engaged in the exegesis of their Scriptures. As believing communities with a body of sacred literature, Judaism and Christianity have continuously sought to understand their Scriptures, to explain their contents, to appropriate their meaning, and to apply and embody their teaching. The manner in which this has been done has varied throughout history. In some respects, however, the history of Judaism and Christianity can be viewed as the history of their interpretation of the Scriptures. Their understanding of the task of interpretation and how this task was to be carried out reflects much about the communities' self-consciousness and their relationship to the culture and thought within which they have found themselves.

Very broadly speaking, the history of biblical exegesis may be divided into three major periods with each of these reflecting particular interests and characteristics. These are (1) the early and medieval period, (2) the period of the Reformation with its roots in late medieval Jewish scholarship and the Renaissance, and (3) the modern period characterized by the attempt to work out clearly defined methods and programs of exegesis. Any such historical scheme must be understood, however, as an oversimplification of a much more complex situation.

(1) The early phase of biblical interpretation was characterized by the assumption that the faith and practices of the communities were identical with and directly authorized by the teachings of the Bible. The faith and practices of the communities were considered divinely ordained. Similarly, the Bible was considered divinely given. Thus, it was presumed that the Bible taught what the communities believed and practiced. Interpreters of the Bible believed themselves to be discerning and

expounding the will and mind of God as these had been given to the biblical writers and embodied in the texts. Everything in the Bible—even difficulties and problems in the text—could be assumed to be revelation. One rabbi advised: "Search it and search it, for everything is in it."

Ancient interpreters recognized that biblical exegesis was a specialized discipline and discussed methods and rules for its interpretation. Rabbi Hillel (d. beginning of the first century A.D.) formulated seven rules for interpreting Scripture and for arguing from Scripture to legal conclusions. These were expanded to thirteen by Rabbi Ishmael in the second century and were subsequently modified and enlarged. The Christian scholar, Tyconius (d. about 400), also drew up seven rules to be used in understanding biblical texts.

Generally, however, the theology of the communities and the interpreters determined the results of the exegesis and interpretation of the Scriptures in this early period. This was especially the case with the Christian use of the Old Testament. In describing methods for interpreting the Bible, Saint Augustine (d. 430), for example, argued the following: "Every student of the Divine Scriptures must exercise himself, having found nothing else in them except, first, that God is to be loved for Himself, and his neighbor for the sake of God; second, that he is to love God with all his heart, with all his soul, and with all his mind; and third, that he should love his neighbor as himself, that is, so that all love for our neighbor should, like all love for ourselves, be referred to God." If a text did not teach this, it was not to be interpreted at face value: "Whatever appears in the divine Word that does not literally pertain to virtuous behavior or to the truth of faith you must take to be figurative." This often meant ignoring the "precise meaning which the author . . . intends to express." He further advised his readers that "when investigation reveals an uncertainty . . . the rule of faith should be consulted as it is found in the more open places of Scripture and in the authority of the Church."

When Augustine talked about taking texts "figuratively," he was referring to the practice of finding a hidden or secondary meaning behind the actual statements and words of Scripture. This practice of finding levels of meanings within texts was widely used in the ancient world. The Stoics had employed such allegorical interpretation so that ancient texts, such as Homer, could be read in a manner that would explain away the unacceptable features in a text and allow the "reading in" of acceptable philosophical and ethical ideas. This approach was greatly developed in the Egyptian city of Alexandria and was applied to the Old Testament by the Jewish exegete Philo (d. about A.D. 50).

The Christian scholar Origen (d. about 254) argued that all biblical texts could have more than one meaning "for just as man consists of body, soul and spirit, so in the same way does the scripture." Some texts, he concluded, since their straightforward meaning did not agree with standard theology or ethics, "have no bodily sense at all, (and) there are occasions when we must seek only for the soul and the spirit, as it were, of the passage." All texts could thus be taken as having a special, secondary spiritual (symbolic, typological, or allegorical) meaning and at times the straightforward meaning could be totally ignored.

This approach could be applied not only to difficult and unedifying texts but also could be used to allegorize other texts. The classical example of this is Augustine's analysis of the parable of the Good Samaritan (Luke 10:29–37). Augustine said the man who went down from Jerusalem to Jericho refers to Adam. Jerusalem is the heavenly city of peace from whose blessedness Adam fell. Jericho means the moon and stands for human mortality, for the moon is born, waxes, wanes, and dies. The thieves who attacked Adam are the devil and his angels. They stripped him of his immortality and beat him by persuading him to sin. They left him half dead. The priest and the Levite who passed the man by without helping him are the priesthood and ministry of the Old Testament which cannot bring salvation. The term Samaritan is taken to mean Guardian, so it refers to Jesus himself. The binding of the wounds is the restraint of sin. Oil is the comfort of good hope and wine is the exhortation to work with fervent spirit. The beast on which the man was placed signifies the flesh in which Christ appeared among men. Being set on the beast means belief in the incarnation of Christ. The inn to which the man is taken is the church where persons are refreshed on their pilgrimage of return to the heavenly city. The two pieces of money that the good Samaritan gave to the innkeeper are the promise of this life and of that to come or else the two main sacraments. The innkeeper is the Apostle Paul.

Not everyone in the early church favored seeking multiple meanings in the interpretation of the text. A group of interpreters, the so-called school of Antioch, advocated a more literal and straightforward reading of the material. They argued that a typological or prophetic reading of an Old Testament text should be engaged in only when it did not do violence to the staightforward meaning.

Eventually, the practice of finding multiple meanings in texts dominated. The standard practice throughout most of the Middle Ages was to exegete so as to discover four meanings in a text: (a) the literal (or

straightforward or historical) meaning, (b) the allegorical (or spiritual-
ized or symbolic) meaning, (c) the tropological (or moral or ethical)
meaning, and (d) the anagogical (or eschatological or heavenly) meaning. A short medieval Latin poem gave expression to this approach:

> The letter shows us what God and our fathers did;
> The allegory shows us where our faith is hid;
> The moral meaning gives us rules of daily life;
> The anagogy shows us where we end our strife.

Jewish exegesis tended to adhere somewhat more closely to the straightforward meaning. This was encouraged by Judaism's less philosophical
theology and a greater desire to follow the explicit edicts and teachings
of the biblical texts. Nonetheless, even Jewish exegesis devised a four-
fold interpretation of texts: (a) *peshat* (the plain meaning), (b)*remez*
(allusion or allegory), (c) *derash* (the homiletical), and (d) *sod* (the mys-
tical or secret).

(2) In the fifteenth and sixteenth centuries, important shifts of perspective occurred in biblical interpretation and exegesis. The impetus for
some of these shifts came from Jewish scholarship of the eleventh and
twelfth centuries. Scholars like Ibn Ezra (d. 1167) and Rashi (d. 1105)
stressed the grammatical analysis of texts which had as its goal the eluci-
dation of the plain meaning (*peshat*) of texts. Renaissance scholars of
the fourteenth and fifteenth centuries rediscovered early classical tradition and texts, and they formulated approaches for their interpretation.

(a) Interpretation broke with the desire to find multiple meanings in
biblical texts while holding to the inspiration of the Scriptures. Martin
Luther (d. 1546), for example, declared: "The Holy Spirit is the plainest
writer and speaker in heaven and earth, and therefore His words cannot
have more than one, and that the very simplest, sense, which we call the
literal, ordinary, natural, sense."

(b) There was a break with traditional interpretation as the best means
of understanding texts. Throughout the Middle Ages, interpretation
often meant nothing more than noting what the church fathers and major
authorities had said about a text. The new impetus tended to bypass tradition in hopes of allowing the texts to speak on their own.

(c) Translations into the common languages meant a break with the
Christian custom of using the Bible only in Latin. This development
raised the problem of which text was to be used in making translations
and stimulated the study of Hebrew and Greek as well as the printing of
texts in the original biblical languages.

(d) The freedom granted interpreters in Protestantism, rather than producing the unanimity of opinion that the reformers had rather naively assumed would result, led instead to a multitude of opinions all believed to be based on sound exegesis and interpretation. Quickly it became obvious that the theological stance and historical situation of the interpreters played an important role in exegesis.

(e) The development of secular learning—philosophy, science, and general humanistic thought—meant that the Bible was no longer taken as the final authority on many matters. Reason came to occupy an important role in human culture and came into conflict with worldviews and systems of thought based on the Bible, revelation, and tradition.

(f) Historical perspectives on all matters, including the Bible, became an important factor. In the medieval world, the past and present tended to blend into a unified whole. There was little sense of the past as past. The past was viewed as an earlier expression of the present. With the development of history as a discipline, the chronological and cultural gaps between the present and the past became more and more obvious. With this came the recognition that the Bible was a book anchored in the past both in origin and in outlook.

(3) The modern period of biblical interpretation, extending from the Enlightenment to the present, may be said to be characterized by one general overall aim: to study and understand the biblical documents as one would any other set of documents from antiquity. Issues such as the historical setting of both the biblical documents and their writers and the role and function of the biblical materials in their original contexts came to the forefront alongside the analysis of their contents. This does not mean that the Bible was not examined for its religious value nor that it was no longer viewed as revelatory material. What happened was that the Bible came to be studied for a variety of reasons and was subjected to a variety of methodological approaches. The Bible could be studied as the means to a number of goals. It could be studied to reconstruct the history and religion of Israel and the early church. It could be studied as the literary remains of early cultures. It could be studied as the foundation documents of two great movements—Judaism and Christianity. It could be studied for its aesthetic and artistic values. These, and other interests, took their place alongside study of the Bible for its religious values and theological insights. The exegetical approaches and procedures which developed to facilitate all of these interests will be the concern of subsequent chapters in this handbook.

The Task of Biblical Exegesis

Exegesis is best thought of as a systematic way of interpreting a text. As noted earlier, everyone engages in exegesis in one form or another, but biblical exegesis has its own specialized needs and disciplines. Its goal, however, is quite simple: to reach an informed understanding of the text. This is different from saying that the exegete seeks to determine *the* meaning of the text. The fact is, there are various aspects of a text's meaning and different types of exegesis can address these different aspects. For this reason, the exegete can never hope to present *the* exegesis of a passage as if it were the final word. Rather, one does *an* exegesis of a passage in which a coherent, informed interpretation is presented, based on one's encounter with and investigation of a text at a given point in time.

To insist on the distinction between "understanding a text" and "establishing *the* meaning of a text" recognizes that an interpreter never fully comprehends a text, especially at one sitting or even at the end of an intensive investigation. This is the reason that exegesis is an ongoing process. It never ceases. Even if one has read a text dozens, even hundreds of times, there will always be dimensions of the text which may come to life in new ways or will be seen from new angles. Exegesis does not allow us to master the text so much as it enables us to enter it.

One way to think about the exegetical task is to conceive of it as learning to interrogate the text. To be sure, the interpreter may not always come to a text with a set of formulated questions, but as one reads a text questions do begin to emerge and intuitions take shape. Doing exegesis requires us to know, first of all, that there are different kinds of questions we can put to a text, and second, which kinds of questions to ask for different purposes. In other words, there are a number of approaches to the study of a text and a number of methods that can be employed to interrogate a text.

We can demonstrate the multiple aspects of exegesis by drawing on a parallel from the study of linguistics. Modern communication theory has developed what is called the "communication triangle" to illustrate the various factors involved in the communication process. The following is a very simplified version of this triangle:

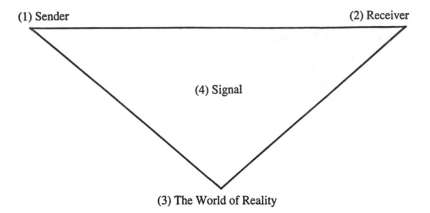

(1) Sender

(2) Receiver

(4) Signal

(3) The World of Reality

In this diagram the sender represents the speaker, writer, artist, or whoever is the originator of communication. The receiver is the audience, listener, hearer, reader, or whoever becomes part of the particular communication process. The world of reality denotes the universe of objects, ideas, and meanings, which are shared in some way by both the sender and receiver and make communication possible. The signal is the means of communication; for the artist it is the work, for a writer it is the text.

A similar schematic diagram constructed and widely used to illustrate the relationship of various literary-critical theories parallels the above communication triangle. This second diagram is as follows:

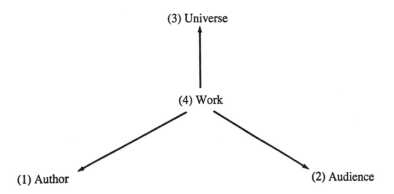

(3) Universe

(4) Work

(1) Author

(2) Audience

If we apply the first model to biblical interpretation, a resulting triangle would look like this:

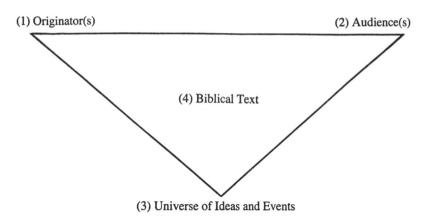

(1) Originator(s)   (2) Audience(s)

(4) Biblical Text

(3) Universe of Ideas and Events

The originator(s) of the biblical text may be an author(s), an editor(s), a redactor, or the community. The audience(s) may be the original or subsequent hearers or readers. The universe of ideas is the shared world of thoughts, perspectives, and understandings that make communication possible and are mirrored and embodied in the text. The text is the medium of communication that may have originally been oral in form but moved to and now encounters us in written form.

In terms of the second diagram above, the relationships in biblical interpretation may be diagrammed as follows:

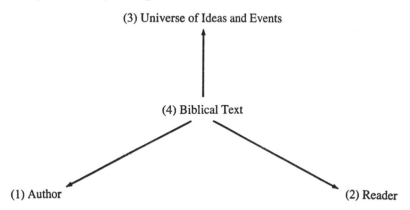

(3) Universe of Ideas and Events

(4) Biblical Text

(1) Author   (2) Reader

The various issues and problems that confront the modern exegete of the text may be viewed in terms of whether the questions we ask focus on one or the other of the components of the model and whether we are concerned with the original or the subsequent components in the process. That is, we can interrogate the text in terms of the author's initial communication, the text's (hypothetical) original shape, the original audience's hearing, understanding, and reception of the communication, and so on. Or we may ask questions about later forms of the text, later audiences, and later understandings realizing we ourselves are now an audience, reading the text in an even later form (generally in translation, for example), and in the context of a universe of ideas that, at least superficially, may differ significantly from those shared by the original participants in the process or those held by subsequent participants in the life of the text.

We do well to remember that the various techniques of biblical criticism have been developed as interpreters have sought to answer particular kinds of questions and to solve particular kinds of problems. In the remainder of this book, we will be discussing the various ways of addressing the questions and problems modern students and interpreters encounter when exegeting the biblical text. The choice is not arbitrary. There is a broad consensus about the kinds of questions to ask, the problems to be encountered, and the methods to be employed. This consensus is the result of centuries of biblical interpretation. Debates still continue about the relative merits of certain types of questions, and they will continue, as they should. Nevertheless, genuine gains in our understanding of the Bible have been made through the use and application of these methods and we should not pretend that we know less than we do. Biblical science has made significant advances, just as has every other field of scientific inquiry. The variety of methods to be discussed merely attests to the richness and diversity of the biblical documents and these methods should be seen as complementary. No single way of approaching a text should be seen as exhausting the meaning of a passage, but rather as a way of dealing with particular facets of a passage.

Each of these approaches is treated as a type of "criticism." This is a technical expression used by scholars to denote a field of study which has developed fairly clearly defined principles and techniques. "Criticism" derives from the Greek word *krinein*, meaning "to judge" or "to discern," and denotes the process through which discerning judgments are made. A literary critic is one who studies literary documents attempting to make intelligent and informed judgments about them. In the end, such judgments may be negative or positive, complimentary or uncomplimentary, but "criticism" per se is a neutral term. Biblical criticism, as a broad category, encompasses many sub-disciplines and a wide variety of interpretive activities which seek to make discerning judgments about the Bible. As such, "being critical" need not mean "being destructive," nor "being constructive" for that matter.

Most of the questions and problems which arise when modern readers engage in exegesis may be classified under one or more of the types of criticism. When a reader discovers an alternative wording within a text and wonders what the orginal wording or what the earliest form of a particular reading might have been, these are the fundamental problems with which *textual criticism* deals. One must determine what the wording of the text to be exegeted is. For this reason, the task of textual criticism is often one of the issues an exegete encounters.

In addition to issues concerning the wording of the passage under consideration, another set of questions arises which has to do with the text's setting in time and space—that is, its historical, geographical, and cultural setting or the context of the original author(s) and audience(s). As noted earlier, if certain customs, events, places, and names are referred to in the text and these are unfamiliar to the reader, they will need to be clarified before understanding results. Not only do matters referred to in the text itself require such clarification, but the history and setting of the text as well. Determining the period, geographical locale, and authorship of the document can be equally important. Such questions as these fall under the rubric of *historical criticism*.

Grammatical criticism includes all attempts to answer questions pertaining to the language of the text. This includes both the words themselves, either alone or in phrases, as well as the way in which the words are put together or the syntax of the sentence or paragraph. Rules of grammar in effect at the time the passage was written may also need to be examined if it appears that meaning and understanding depend upon resolving grammatical issues.

Concern with the style, character, compositional techniques, and rhetorical patterns constitutes the field of *literary criticism*. (Frequently, in biblical studies, literary criticism has been too narrowly identified with source analysis, which comprises only one aspect of literary criticism.) Such matters as the location of a passage within larger literary units and how the passage functions within these larger units are often quite crucial in understanding and interpreting a text. Since most of the biblical documents were originally oral in form or else written to be read aloud and were intended to persuade a listening audience, ancient authors like ancient orators were ordinarily intentional and careful about how they put together and arranged their compositions. Thus the rhetorical features of a text must be given careful consideration.

If literary criticism deals with how the passage is structured and how it relates to its larger literary unit, *form criticism* is more narrowly concerned with the passage itself or with sub-units in a passage. Special attention is given to the literary form or genre of the passage, for example, whether it is a parable, a prophetic speech, a hymn, and so forth. Attention to these questions has arisen because of the recognition that form and meaning are directly related; one reads a poem one way, a piece of prose another. The Bible contains a rich diversity of literary forms and genres and many of these already existed prior to their actual appearance in the biblical text. For this reason, questions of the original setting of particular literary forms and genres are also crucial as one seeks to determine the "life situation" of a passage.

It is now widely recognized that the Bible, in many of its parts, resembles an anthology of sacred writings where revered stories, traditions, and sayings uttered by individuals and preserved by various communities have been collected, edited, and formed into a single text. This means that some texts have a "pre-history," by which is meant that they were actually spoken or written, preserved and transmitted much earlier than their incorporation into the biblical text itself. Efforts to uncover the earlier stages of development through which a text has passed are dealt with under *tradition criticism*.

Even though a text might have a pre-history, the reader finds it located within a specific biblical writing. Thus the interpreter will also want to ask how the author(s) or editor(s) intended a passage to be understood in its final literary form. *Redaction criticism* focuses on the final form of the passage and on the changes or redactions it may have undergone in the editorial process. It assesses the significance of these editorial changes and reshapings, which may have occurred in the various written stages prior to and including its final form.

The biblical text, like any other, may be read and interpreted purely as a text without regard to such historically oriented matters as the text's origins, the author's intention, and the original audience. Such an approach focuses on the structure and meaning of the text in light of universal concerns and factors, as these are encountered in and brought to the text by the reader. *Structural criticism*, as this approach is called, has recently been borrowed from general criticism and applied to biblical texts. Such criticism seeks to explain how meaning is structured into a text, to understand how a reader comprehends a text, and to discover how universal structures of thought open the text to the reader.

Over the centuries, the Bible has been and continues to be read as sacred Scripture. As Scripture, the Bible, in varying forms, constitutes a canon for Jewish and Christian communities of faith. *Canonical criticism* explores how the Scriptures were transmitted and shaped by believing communities to produce a canon and how texts are to be read and understood as parts of a collection of sacred writings.

By arranging these various aspects of the exegetical process in this order, we do not mean to suggest that exegesis is a mechanical undertaking which one can accomplish in a stair-step order as if one method or stage of exegesis always leads to the next. Normally, questions may arise from the text in an unsystematic order, depending on the nature of the text. For example, an interpreter may be puzzled first by literary or historical features of a text and only later discover that an important textual variant within the passage needs to be clarified. Even though questions may arise from the text in a somewhat random fashion, they need not be pursued randomly. Instead, the interpreter will discover that fairly systematic ways of tackling various exegetical questions do exist and that they may be pursued to achieve good results.

Generally speaking, the exegetical task may be said to fall into two fairly clearly defined stages: analysis and synthesis. As the interpreter begins the task of exegesis, examining different aspects of the passage, whether they are historical, grammatical, literary, or whatever, will serve as a way of ''breaking down'' the passage into its component parts and problems and examining them as discrete units and issues. These separate analytic tasks will normally interlock for each will inform the other. As analysis takes place, the interpreter's understanding of the passage will gradually increase and the groundwork will be laid for synthesis. By synthesis, we mean the process by which the interpreter again ''puts together'' the text. Here, the task is to relate the preliminary analytical investigations to each other, weighing the significance of each, and deciding how they contribute to the overall interpretation.

As exegesis takes place, the interpreter will discover that exegesis has both a positive and negative function. Positively, the interpreter will be able to establish certain matters about the text that were previously unknown or uncertain, and as a result, the exegetical task produces new knowledge, at least for the interpreter. Negatively, the interpreter may succeed in determining only what the text cannot mean. Quite often, the most productive part of exegesis is uncovering ''false understandings'' or ways of looking at the text which do not conform to the evidence and insight discovered in an examination of the text through the exegetical process. To put it another way, the exegete may succeed only in drawing further limits around the passage or in narrowing the concentric circles of meaning and interpretation which have grown up around the text in the history of interpretation. Although this may cause the interpreter to become more modest, it is scarcely a negligible accomplishment.

In every case, the interpreter will soon discover that, although employing the tools, methods, and findings of well-developed disciplines, such as lexicography, textual criticism, and historical analysis, exegesis is nevertheless an art as well as a science. It requires both imagination and creativity, not only in learning how to put questions to a text, but also in learning how to answer them, and above all in synthesizing these answers into a coherent, meaningful interpretation of the passage. Contrary to popular opinion, however, one can learn to be an artist as well as a scientist.

BIBLIOGRAPHY

(Items marked with an asterisk are especially recommended as additional reading for beginning students.)

Bibliographies

Bollier, J., *The Literature of Theology: A Guide for Students and Pastors* (Philadelphia: Westminster Press, 1979).

*Childs, B. S., *Old Testament Books for Pastor and Teacher* (Philadelphia: Westminster Press, 1977).

Danker, F. W., *Multipurpose Tools for Bible Study* (3d ed.; St. Louis: Concordia Publishing House, 1970).

*Fitzmyer, J. A., *An Introductory Bibliography for the Study of Scripture* (rev. ed.; Rome: Biblical Institute Press, 1981).

France, R. T., *A Bibliographical Guide to New Testament Research* (3d ed.; Sheffield: JSOT Press, 1979).

Hurd, J. C., Jr., *A Bibliography of New Testament Bibliographies* (New York: Seabury Press, 1966).

Marrow, S. B., *Basic Tools of Biblical Exegesis* (Rome: Biblical Institute Press, 1978).

*Martin, R. P., *New Testament Books for Pastor and Teacher* (Philadelphia: Westminster Press, 1984).

Scholer, D. M., *A Basic Bibliographic Guide for New Testament Exegesis* (2d ed.; Grand Rapids: Eerdmans Publishing Company, 1973).

Wagner, G. (ed.), *An Exegetical Bibliography of the New Testament* (Macon: Mercer University Press, 1982–).

Biblical Exegesis

*Barton, J., *Reading the Old Testament: Method in Biblical Study* (London/Philadelphia: Darton, Longman and Todd/Westminster Press, 1984).

Barton, J., "Classifying Biblical Criticism " in *Journal for the Study in Old Testament* 29 (1984) 19–35.

Blackman, E. C., "The Task of Exegesis" in *The Background of the New Testament and Its Eschatology* (ed. by W. D. Davies and D. Daube; London: Cambridge University Press, 1964) 3–26.

Brown, R. E., *Biblical Exegesis and Church Doctrine* (New York: Paulist Press, 1985).

Bultmann, R., "Is Exegesis Without Presuppositions Possible?" in *New Testament and Mythology and Other Basic Writings: Rudolf Bultmann* (ed. by S. M. Ogden; Philadelphia/London: Fortress Press/SCM Press, 1984/1985) 145–53.

Carson, D. A., *Exegetical Fallacies* (Grand Rapids: Baker Book House, 1984).

Cullmann, O., "The Necessity and Function of Higher Criticism" in *The Early Church* (ed. by A. J. B. Higgins; London/Philadelphia: SCM Press/Westminster Press, 1956) 3–16.

Doty, W. G., *Contemporary New Testament Interpretation* (Englewood Cliffs: Prentice-Hall, 1972).

Fee, G. D., *New Testament Exegesis: A Handbook for Students and Pastors* (Philadelphia: Westminster Press, 1983).

*Furnish, V. P., "Some Practical Guidelines for New Testament Exegesis" in *Perkins School of Theology Journal 26* (1973) 1–16.

Kaiser, O. and W. G. Kümmel, *Exegetical Method: A Student's Handbook* (rev. ed.; New York: Seabury Press, 1981).

Kaiser, W. C., *Toward an Exegetical Theology: Biblical Exegesis for Preaching and Teaching* (Grand Rapids: Baker Book House, 1981).

*Keck, L. E. and G. M. Tucker, "Exegesis" in *Interpreter's Dictionary of the Bible, Supplementary Volume* (Nashville: Abingdon Press, 1976) 296–303.

Malherbe, A. J., "An Introduction: The Task and Method of Exegesis " in *Restoration Quarterly* 5 (1961) 169–78.

Marshall, I. H. (ed.), *New Testament Interpretation: Essays on Principles and Methods* (Exeter/Grand Rapids: Paternoster Press/Eerdmans Publishing Company, 1977/1978).

Mays, J. L., *Exegesis as a Theological Discipline* (Richmond: Union Theological Seminary, 1960).

Reumann, J., "Methods in Studying the Biblical Text Today" in *Concordia Theological Monthly 40* (1969) 655–81.

Stuart, D., *Old Testament Exegesis: A Primer for Students and Pastors* (rev. ed.; Philadelphia: Westminster Press, 1984).

Yoder, P., *From Word to Life: A Guide to the Art of Bible Study* (Scottdale, PA/ Kitchener, ONT: Herald Press, 1982).

History of Biblical Interpretation

Ackroyd, P. R. et al. (eds.), *Cambridge History of the Bible* (3 vols.; London/ New York: Cambridge University Press, 1963–1970).

Benson, J. E., "The History of the Historical-Critical Method in the Church " in *Dialog* 12 (1973) 94–103.

Blackman, E. C., *Biblical Interpretation* (London/Philadelphia: Independent Press/Westminster Press, 1957).

Bovon, F. and G. Rouiller, *Exegesis: Problems of Method and Exercises in Reading (Genesis 22 and Luke 15)* (Pittsburgh/Edinburgh: Pickwick Press/T. & T. Clark, 1978).

Bruce, F. F., "The History of New Testament Study " in I. H. Marshall (ed.), *New Testament Interpretation*, pp. 21–59.

*Clements, R. E., *One Hundred Years of Old Testament Interpretation = A Century of Old Testament Study* (rev. ed.; Philadelphia/London: Westminster Press/Lutterworth Press, 1983).

Ebeling, G., "The Significance of the Critical Historical Method for Church and Theology in Protestantism" in his *Word and Faith* (Philadelphia/London: Fortress Press/SCM Press, 1963) 17–61.

Evans, G. R., *The Language and Logic of the Bible: The Earlier Middle Ages* (Cambridge/New York: Cambridge University Press, 1984).

Evans, G. R., *The Language and Logic of the Bible: The Road to Reformation* (Cambridge/New York: Cambridge University Press, 1985).

Fishbane, M., *Biblical Interpretation in Ancient Israel* (Oxford/New York: Oxford University Press, 1986).

Froehlich, K., *Biblical Interpretation in the Early Church* (Philadelphia: Fortress Press, 1985).

*Grant, R. M., with D. Tracy, *A Short History of the Interpretation of the Bible* (rev. ed.; Philadelphia/London: Fortress Press/SCM Press, 1984).

*Greenspahn, F. E. (ed.), *Scripture in the Jewish and Christian Traditions: Authority, Interpretation, Relevance* (Nashville: Abingdon Press, 1982).

Hahn, H. F., *The Old Testament in Modern Research* (2d ed.; Philadelphia/London: Fortress Press/SCM Press, 1966).

Henry, P., *New Directions in New Testament Study* (Philadelphia/London: Westminster Press/SCM Press, 1979).

Krentz, E., *The Historical-Critical Method* (Philadelphia/London: Fortress Press/SPCK, 1975).

Kümmel, W. G., *The New Testament: The History of the Investigation of Its Problems* (Nashville/London: Abingdon Press/SCM Press, 1972).

Kugel, J. L. and R. A. Greer, *Early Biblical Interpretation* (Philadelphia/London: Westminster Press/SPCK, 1986/1987).

*Neill, S., *The Interpretation of the New Testament, 1861–1961* (London/New York: Oxford University Press, 1964).

Reventlow, H. G., *The Authority of the Bible and the Rise of the Modern World* (London/Philadelphia: SCM Press/Fortress Press, 1984).

Rogers, J. B. and D. K. McKim, *The Authority and Interpretation of the Bible: An Historical Approach* (San Francisco/London: Harper & Row, 1979).

Rogerson, J., *Old Testament Criticism in the Nineteenth Century: England and Germany* (London/Philadelphia: SPCK/Fortress Press, 1984).

Smalley, B., *The Study of the Bible in the Middle Ages* (rev. ed.; Notre Dame: University of Notre Dame Press, 1964).

Weingreen, J. et al., "Interpretation, History of" in *Interpreter's Dictionary of the Bible, Supplementary Volume*, 436–56.

Wood, J. D., *The Interpretation of the Bible* (London: Gerald Duckworth & Co. Ltd., 1958).

CHAPTER 2

TEXTUAL CRITICISM:

The Quest for the Original Wording

When studying a biblical text, the interpreter frequently encounters different wordings, or variant readings, for the same passage. This may be noticed when one reads the same passage in different translations. For example, reading the story of the conversion of the Ethiopian nobleman in Acts 8 in the King James Version, one notices the nobleman's confession given in verse 37. Reading the same account in the Revised Standard Version, one discovers that the confession is missing from the text. Instead, it is placed in a footnote and prefaced with the remark: "Other ancient authorities add all or most of verse 37."

Variant wordings of a passage may also be noticed if one is working with a single translation, particularly if it is an edition of one of the major committee translations of the Bible, such as the Revised Standard Version (RSV), The New English Bible (NEB), The Jerusalem Bible (JB), the New Jewish Version (NJV), The New International Version (NIV), or the New American Bible (NAB). Reading a passage in such a modern edition, the interpreter may be referred to a footnote and be met with a list of symbols and abbreviations. For example, in the RSV, in the text of Micah 1:5, one reads: "And what is the sin of the house^a of Judah?" In the footnote indicated by the supralinear "a," one reads: "Gk Tg Compare Syr: Heb *what are the high places*." This indicates that the wording given in the translation is taken from the Greek translation (Gk) and the Targums (Tg; Aramaic translations) and is similar to what is found in the Syriac translation (Syr) although the Hebrew reads *what are the high places*. Or, in reading Genesis 10:5, the reader is referred to a note which says: "Compare verses 20, 31. Heb lacks *These are the sons of Japheth*." This footnote indicates that the added material does not appear in the Hebrew nor in any ancient translation but has been added by the translators on the assumption that this statement, by analogy with verses 20 and 31, had dropped out of the text. Notations such as these appear frequently enough in modern translations of the Bible for the interpreter to ask: what accounts for these variations of wording within a text? which of the variants represents the original reading? or, can one even determine the original wording of a text?

An understanding of the nature of our earliest biblical manuscripts can help one to appreciate why such notations occur, what they mean, and how to use them. None of the original manuscripts, or autographs, of any biblical writing has been preserved. For that matter, so far as we know, not even first or secondhand copies of any of the original manuscripts have survived. What has survived are copies of copies, handwritten by scribes. Some of these copies are more ancient than others, but the oldest are usually copies of individual books or only fragments or parts of books. The oldest surviving manuscript of a portion of the Old Testament so far discovered dates from the third century B.C., while the earliest extant New Testament manuscript is a fragment from the Gospel of John dating from the early second century A.D. This means that, with respect to every single biblical writing, there exists a chronological gap between the original manuscript written by a biblical author or compiled by an editor and the earliest preserved copy. Thus, it is probably an illusion to assume that we can ever recover with certainty the "original" wording of a biblical text.

Thousands of copies of biblical writings, however, have been preserved from ancient times. Some of these are complete manuscripts containing the entire Hebrew Old Testament or Greek New Testament or major portions of each. Many others are manuscripts of individual books. Still others are manuscripts containing only portions of single books. No two of these manuscripts, however, are identical in every detail.

As early as the third century B.C., the Old Testament began to be translated into Greek and later was translated into other languages, including Syriac and Latin. The New Testament also, shortly after it was written, began to be translated, first into Syriac, later into Latin. It also appeared in other lesser known languages, such as Coptic, an Egyptian dialect. Often manuscripts of these translations, even in the same language, differ significantly from one another.

In addition, the contents of some ancient translations of Old Testament materials differ radically from Hebrew manuscripts. For example, the Hebrew version of Job is one-sixth longer than the Greek version and the Greek version of Jeremiah is about one-eighth shorter than the Hebrew version with much of the material appearing in a different order.

Because of the popularity of the biblical writings, they were often quoted in commentaries and other written works which dealt with biblical topics. Often such quotations differ from one another and from known manuscripts in the original and translated languages.

Thus we possess four types of textual variants for biblical materials: (1) variations among manuscripts in the original languages, (2) variations among manuscripts in early translations, (3) variations between ancient manuscripts in the original languages and manuscripts of early translations, and (4) variant quotations in early Jewish and Christian writings.

Once the student understands not only how ancient writings were originally composed but also how they were copied, preserved, transmitted, translated and quoted, it is easier to understand how and why such variations in the wording of a biblical passage could result.

Many of the varying quotations in rabbinical and early Christian literature arose because writers were frequently quoting from memory. Major differences between early translations and original-language manuscripts, as in the case of Job and Jeremiah, probably resulted because different textual traditions or different versions of these books lie behind the surviving Greek and Hebrew texts. In some cases, the Greek texts may be closer to the original than the known Hebrew texts.

Textual variants within manuscripts of the original biblical languages are frequently due to ''corruptions'' of the text. Generally speaking, textual critics have detected two kinds of corruptions which occur in the transmission of ancient texts and which produce variant readings: (a) unintentional and (b) intentional. Unintentional errors include those mistakes copyists would make either in wrongly hearing a text or in wrongly reading a text. One way copies could be produced quickly in the ancient world was for a single person to read the text aloud while a roomful of scribes wrote copies. As welcome and efficient as this earliest form of multiple copying might have been, there was always the possibility for hearing errors to occur. The copyist might not hear the word read correctly and thus write something else. Or, having heard correctly, the copyist might not write exactly what was heard. Or, even when a scribe was copying a manuscript by looking at one document and making a written copy, visual errors also occurred. The scribe might, for example, skip a word or a line, write a word or a line twice, misspell a word, reverse the order of letters within a single word, or reverse the order of words within a sentence. Sometimes notes or glosses made in the margins of early texts were taken as part of the texts themselves and incorporated into the text by later copyists. These are only some of the ways unintentional errors might occur.

Intentional changes in the wording in the text could occur for a variety of reasons. A scribe might feel compelled to correct the spelling or grammar of a manuscript being copied, and regardless of whether the correction was right or wrong, this would introduce yet another variation into the textual tradition. The scribe might also choose to rearrange the order of words, sentences, or even paragraphs, and on occasion add material if there was a felt need to do so. This may have been done to produce a more coherent or a more logically sequential account. In any event, such changes, transpositions, and glosses were made by scribes, even when they were copying sacred texts. Although we may now be able to determine that their "correction" was wrong, they at least thought they were improving the text. Scribes also changed texts intentionally for theological or doctrinal reasons. If the text being copied contained a statement with which the scribe disagreed, it was sometimes changed or expanded to be brought into conformity with a more orthodox position. Ancient Hebrew scribes, for example, noted at least eighteen cases in which they had changed the text for theological reasons. In some cases, the scribe might choose simply to omit the offensive verse or passage. Whenever intentional changes were made in the text—and they were made for other reasons as well—they were made in the hopes of improving the text or its content.

Ancient biblical writings were copied frequently and became widespread throughout the Mediterranean world. As one might expect, certain centers, usually major cities such as Alexandria or Rome, became the "home" of certain biblical texts either because early copies might have been preserved there or because the names of revered biblical personalities or scribes came to be associated with such cities. It is not difficult to imagine how a definite type of textual tradition might originate and develop within one geographical locale. Scholars have, in fact, examined the many remaining copies of the biblical writings, especially the New Testament and the Greek versions of the Old Testament, and have assigned them to families or recensions, based on their similarities as well as their attachment to certain geographical locales. Although not every extant biblical manuscript will fit into these families, they are distinct enough to provide a convenient way of grouping the manuscrips which have been preserved, especially in the case of the New Testament. They are grouped in families because of their genealogical relationship. If a particular textual variant was introduced, let us say, in the fourth century A.D., and this same variant was repeated in an entire "set" of manuscripts, and if this tendency repeated itself enough times, this would constitute sufficient evidence to group all the manuscripts showing similar characteristics into the same family. Moreover, as scholars have studied the various tendencies within families of manuscripts, they have noted certain characteristics. Some manuscript families tend to be expansionist because they will consistently contain variant readings which are longer than those in other groupings. Other manuscript families, by contrast, may be more conservative in that they exhibit reluctance to include any changes, either expansions or reductions in wording. Knowing this becomes valuable to the exegete when assessing the relative merits of particular variants. For example, if a variant reading occurs in the text and it is found to be supported only by a manuscript or a group of manuscripts with an expansionist tendency, it will more likely be discounted, all other things being equal.

As the science of textual criticism has developed over the centuries, our knowledge of the process by which early manuscripts have been preserved and transmitted has increased dramatically. In addition, detailed knowledge of particular manuscripts, such as their date and place of origin, peculiarities of style, and how they relate to other manuscripts has been accumulated. Archaeological discoveries, such as the discovery of the Qumran or Dead Sea scrolls, have also provided valuable information for textual criticism. The results of these scholarly activities continue to be available in books and periodicals, but they come to fruition perhaps most visibly in the production of critical editions of the biblical writings and in the modern translations produced by committees of scholars using such critical editions.

A critical edition of any ancient writing, including the Old and New Testaments, contains a text in the original language in which the writing was produced, along with an extensive set of footnotes, the critical apparatus, which lists textual variants and the different ancient sources in which the various readings have been preserved, including ancient manuscripts, translations, versions, and the works of early commentators and scholars. Some critical editions provide only a selection of all the textual variants, while others attempt to include every variation within the text. Although modern committee translations do not reproduce the text in the original language, they nevertheless have been produced by scholars who have given close attention to textual-critical matters. None of the modern translations contains an extensive critical apparatus. They rather provide footnotes indicating the most important variations in wording and give some indication of the nature of the variation. In an abbreviated fashion, they indicate for the reader the type of variation, whether addition, omission, alteration, or transposition and indicate in what textual traditions these occur. The latest critical editions of the Hebrew and Greek texts, and the latest committee translations of the Bible, both Old and New Testaments, provide the most up-to-date accumulation of the results of textual critics working with biblical texts. These are perhaps the most natural final form into which the work of textual critics is cast.

As the exegete encounters variants within the text, the primary task will be to examine the variants, assess their relative importance, and decide how they affect the passage to be interpreted. Naturally, the beginning student will need to rely on the work of experts since textual criticism itself is a highly developed and complex science. Even so, it is important to understand what textual criticism seeks to achieve and how it works. Essentially, textual criticism has a threefold aim: (a) to determine the process by which a text has been transmitted and has come to exist in variant forms; (b) to establish the original wording, when this is judged to be possible or feasible; and (c) to determine the best form and wording of the text that the modern reader should use.

Various criteria for assessing variant readings have been developed by textual critics. In spite of their complexity, they are often based on common sense and ingenuity. By familiarizing themselves with what happens when ancient texts were composed, copied, preserved, and transmitted, textual critics have detected the kinds of changes that occur. They have also established the reasons why such changes occur. Consequently, the criteria for judging these changes often consist in "working back" from the variants toward the more original form of the text. For example, one of the most fundamental axioms with which textual critics work is this: "The more difficult reading is to be preferred." This rule is based on the observation that scribes tended to smooth out difficulties rather than create them. Consequently, given two variations of wording, the more difficult reading is more likely to have given rise to the simpler reading rather than vice versa. Another general rule is: "The shorter reading is to be preferred." Because copyists tended to be expansionist rather than reductionist, textual critics will generally give priority to a shorter reading rather than a longer one, since they have discovered that scribes were more likely to have made additions to the text rather than deletions. In similar fashion, scribes tended to harmonize divergent readings rather than create them. For this reason, a variant which looks "harmonistic" tends to be discounted in favor of one which creates a dissonance of some sort. In addition to these scribal tendencies, textual critics also take into account matters of style, vocabulary, and literary context. For example, if a variant reading tends not to conform to the author's vocabulary and style as used elsewhere in the same document or if it does not easily fit into the larger literary context of the document, then the likelihood of its being a corruption is increased.

All of the above considerations arise from within the text itself, and thus are regarded as "internal evidence." When considerations are brought to bear from outside the text, these are classified as "external evidence." This evidence includes such matters as the date and character of the manuscript witnesses, the geographical distribution of the manuscript witnesses, and the genealogical relationship between the various families of texts. As noted earlier, textual critics have classified most of the manuscript witnesses into types or families. They have also established both dates and geographical locales for the manuscripts. In some instances, the manuscripts contain this information; in other instances, it has to be deduced from other considerations, such as the style of writing, the type of material on which the manuscript was written, and so forth. Lists of the relevant manuscripts, with their assigned dates and locations, are contained in critical editions, and are easily available in standard works.

The types of considerations at work here often involve chronology. If a variant reading occurs, one of the first questions to be asked is: When did it enter the manuscript tradition? Was it original or not? If not, was it an early or late change? Generally speaking, the earlier a reading, the more likely it is to be authentic. Yet, because of what we know about the transmission of manuscripts, this is not invariably the case. For example, a corrupt reading might be attested in a fourth-century manuscript, while an eighth-century manuscript might preserve a better tradition and the original reading. In this case, obviously, the later reading is to be preferred. Similarly, if a corrupt reading is attested in several extant manuscripts, whereas a clearly authentic reading is attested in only one extant manuscript, the latter would be preferred, even though supported by only one manuscript witness. Hence, another general rule developed by textual critics is that manuscript witnesses are to be weighed rather than counted.

It can now be seen that in deciding between readings no single criterion will work in every case, for some offset others. Instead, the textual critic begins with a particular instance, accumulates all the evidence possible, both internal and external, then examines and assesses the problem on its individual merits. All of the criteria are brought to bear on the problem, but in the end it is the textual critic's own informed judgment, and in many instances creative insight, which tilts the balance one way or another.

As the beginning student becomes more familiar with the study of texts, what these criteria are and how they are applied will become clearer. Such understanding will allow the student to make more sense of the critical apparatus in modern critical editions as well as modern translations.

At this point, however, it is in order to suggest a procedure which the beginning student can follow in addressing textual-critical problems which arise in a biblical passage. First, the text and the footnotes in a modern committee translation, or preferably several translations, should be consulted. These are usually located at the bottom of the page and generally only note the most important textual problems. In annotated translations, they are directly above the explanatory notes, which usually deal with other matters. Second, one should determine the type of problem involved. Any abbreviations or symbols used in the textual-critical notes will be explained in the preface of the edition being used, and by consulting these, the student will be able to determine more precisely the nature of the problem. Third, having done so, the student should consult a critical commentary on the passage. A critical commentary, as opposed to a more general, expository commentary, will mention all the important textual-critical problems and discuss them. Even though critical commentaries will employ Hebrew and Greek terms, the student who possesses knowledge of neither original language will be able to determine the gist of the problem. If the translators of a particular edition have produced a handbook explaining their choice of various readings, these should also be consulted. On the basis of these, and perhaps after having consulted more than one commentary, the student should take a fourth step. This will require listing the variants and, beside each variant, a listing of the supporting witnesses. Once this is done, one will need to apply the external criteria, that is, determine how early the witnesses are which attest the various readings, and how much stock one should place in them. One may then begin to apply the internal criteria, asking whether a particular reading conforms to the general expectations of the document based on what is known about it internally. For example, is it consistent with the style, vocabulary, context, and theology of the rest of the document? Or, is a reading simpler or more difficult, shorter or longer? Quite often, valuable discussions of important passages are contained in books devoted to texual criticism, and the student should check the index of biblical references in some of the standard volumes to find these.

Obviously, the ability to pursue textual-critical questions is increased if one possesses a knowledge of the original languages. In this case, one should first consult one of the standard critical editions of the Bible. One can then lay out the alternative readings and see the nature of the problem, and then proceed to collect and assess the evidence. For external criteria, lists of the manuscripts and their characteristics are readily available, and these should be consulted as one itemizes the manuscript witnesses supporting each variant. In close conjunction with this, the critical commentaries should be consulted, and from them a more informed understanding of the problem can be reached and decisions can be made about the variant readings.

BIBLIOGRAPHY

Critical Editions of the Old Testament

Brooke, A. E. et al. (eds.), *The Old Testament in Greek* (3 vols.; London: Cambridge University Press, 1906–1940). Incomplete.

Elliger, K. and W. Rudolph (eds.), *Biblia hebraica stuttgartensia* (Stuttgart: Deutsche Bibelstiftung, 1977).

Kittel, R. (ed.), *Biblia hebraica* (9th ed.; Stuttgart: Württembergische Bibelanstalt, 1954).

Rahlfs, A. (ed.), *Septuaginta* (8th ed.; 2 vols.; Stuttgart: Württembergische Bibelanstalt, 1965).

Septuaginta: Vetus Testamentum graece auctoritate Societatis Göttingensis editum (Göttingen: Vandenhoeck & Ruprecht, 1931–).

Critical Editions of the New Testament

Aland, K. et al. (eds.), *The Greek New Testament* (3d ed.; New York/London: United Bible Societies, 1975).

Aland, K. (ed.), *Synopsis quattuor evangeliorum: Locis parallelis evangeliorum apocryphorum et patrum adhibitis* (9th ed.; Stuttgart: Deutsche Bibelstiftung, 1976).

Aland K. (ed), *Synopsis of the Four Gospels: Greek-English Edition of the Synopsis Quattuor Evangeliorum with the Text of the Revised Standard Version* (3d ed.; New York/London: United Bible Societies, 1979).

Funk, R. W., *New Gospel Parallels* (2 vols.; Philadelphia: Fortress Press, 1985–1987).

Greeven, H. (ed.), *Synopse der drei ersten Evangelien: mit Beigabe der johannei-*

schen Parallelstellen = *Synopsis of the First Three Gospels with the Addition of the Johannine Parallels* (Tübingen: J. C. B. Mohr [Paul Siebeck], 1981).

Huck, A. (ed.), *Synopsis of the First Three Gospels* (9th ed., rev. by H. Lietzmann; Tübingen: J. C. B. Mohr [Paul Siebeck], 1950; English ed. by F. L. Cross; Oxford: Basil Blackwell, 1957).

Kilpatrick, G. D. (ed.), *Hē kainē diathēkē* (2d ed.; London: British and Foreign Bible Society, 1958).

Nestle, E. and K. Aland (eds.), *Novum Testamentum Graece* (26th ed.; Stuttgart: Deutsche Bibelstiftung, 1979).

Throckmorton, B. H., Jr., *Gospel Parallels: A Synopsis of the First Three Gospels* (4th ed.; New York/London: Thomas Nelson, 1979).

Old Testament Textual Criticism

*Ap-Thomas, D. R., *A Primer of Old Testament Text Criticism* (2d ed.; Oxford: Basil Blackwell, 1965).

Cross, F. M. and S. Talmon (eds.), *Qumran and the History of the Biblical Text* (Cambridge/London: Harvard University Press, 1975).

Jellicoe, S., *The Septuagint and Modern Study* (London/New York: Oxford University Press, 1968; reprinted, Ann Arbor: Eisenbrauns, 1978).

Jellicoe, S. (ed.), *Studies in the Septuagint: Origins, Recensions, and Interpretations: Selected with a Prolegomenon* (New York: KTAV, 1974).

Klein, R. W., *Textual Criticism of the Old Testament: The Septuagint After Qumran* (Philadelphia: Fortress Press, 1974).

Leiman, S. Z. (ed.), *The Canon and Masorah of the Hebrew Bible* (New York: KTAV, 1974).

*McCarter, P. K., Jr., *Textual Criticism: Recovering the Text of the Hebrew Bible* (Philadelphia: Fortress Press, 1986).

Roberts, B. J., *The Old Testament Text and Versions: The Hebrew Text in Transmission and the History of the Ancient Versions* (Cardiff: University of Wales Press, 1951).

Roberts, B. J., "The Textual Transmission of the Old Testament" in *Tradition and Interpretation* (ed. by G. W. Anderson; London/New York: Oxford University Press, 1979) 1–30.

Tov, E., *The Text-Critical Use of the Septuagint in Biblical Research* (Jerusalem: Simor Ltd., 1981).

*Weingreen, J., *Introduction to the Critical Study of the Text of the Hebrew Bible* (London/New York: Oxford University Press, 1982).

Wonneberger, R., *Understanding BHS: A Manual for the Users of Biblia hebraica stuttgartensia* (Rome: Pontifical Institute Press, 1984).

Würthwein, E., *The Text of the Old Testament: An Introduction to the Biblia Hebraica* (rev. ed.; Grand Rapids/London: Eerdmans Publishing Company/ SCM Press, 1979).

New Testament Textual Criticism

*Aland, K. and B. Aland, *The Text of the New Testament* (Leiden/Grand Rapids: E. J. Brill/Eerdmans Publishing Company, 1987).

Birdsall, J. N., "The New Testament Text" in *Cambridge History of the Bible*, 1. 308–77.

Colwell, E. C., *What is the Best New Testament?* (Chicago: University of Chicago Press, 1952).

Colwell, E. C., *Studies in Methodology in Textual Criticism of the New Testament* (Leiden/Grand Rapids: E. J. Brill/Eerdmans Publishing Company, 1969).

Epp, E. J., "The Eclectic Method in New Testament Textual Criticism: Solution or Symptom?" in *Harvard Theological Review* 69 (1976) 211–57.

Epp, E. J. and G. D. Fee (eds.), *New Testament Textual Criticism: Its Significance for Exegesis* (London/New York: Oxford University Press, 1981).

*Fee, G. D., "The Textual Criticism of New Testament " in *Biblical Criticism: Historical, Literary, and Textual* (ed. by R. K. Harrison et al.; Grand Rapids: Zondervan Publishing House, 1978) 127–55.

Finegan, J., *Encountering New Testament Manuscripts: A Working Introduction to Textual Criticism* (Grand Rapids/London: Eerdmans Publishing Company/ SPCK, 1974/1975).

Greenlee, J. H., *Introduction to New Testament Textual Criticism* (Grand Rapids: Eerdmans Publishing Company, 1964).

Hatch, W. H. P., *Facsimiles and Descriptions of Minuscule Manuscripts of the New Testament* (Cambridge: Harvard University Press, 1951).

Hatch, W. H. P., *The Principal Uncial Manuscripts of the New Testament* (Chicago: University of Chicago Press, 1939).

Kenyon, F. G., *The Text of the Greek Bible* (3rd ed., rev.; London: Gerald Duckworth and Co., 1982).

Metzger, B. M., *The Early Versions of the New Testament: Their Origin, Transmission, and Limitations* (London/New York: Oxford University Press, 1977).

*Metzger, B. M., *The Text of the New Testament: Its Transmission, Corruption, and Restoration* (2d ed.; New York/London: Oxford University Press, 1968).

Metzger, B. M., *A Textual Commentary on the Greek New Testament* (London/ New York: United Bible Societies, 1971).

Moulton, H. K., *Papyrus, Parchment and Print: The Story of How the New Testament Text Has Reached Us* (London: Lutterworth Press, 1967).

Roberts, C. H., "Books in the Graeco-Roman World and in the New Testament" in *Cambridge History of the Bible*, 1. 48–66.

Tasker, R. V. G. (ed.), *The Greek New Testament: Being the Text Translated in the New English Bible, 1961* (London/New York: Oxford University Press/ Cambridge University Press, 1964).

Taylor, V., *The Text of the New Testament: A Short Introduction* (London/New York: Macmillan and Co. Ltd./St. Martin's Press, 1961).

Translation and History of the Bible

Arbez, E., "Modern Translations of the Old Testament: V. English Language Translations" in *Catholic Biblical Quarterly* 17 (1955) 456–85.

*Bailey, L. R. (ed.), *The Word of God: A Guide to English Versions of the Bible* (Atlanta: John Knox Press, 1982).

Brenton, L. C. L. (ed.), *The Septuagint with Apocrypha: Greek and English* (London: Samuel Bagster & Sons, 1851; reprinted, Grand Rapids: Zondervan Publishing House, 1970).

Brockington, L. H. (ed.), *The Hebrew Text of the Old Testament: The Readings*

Adopted by the Translators of the New English Bible (London/New York: Oxford University Press/Cambridge University Press, 1973).

Bruce, F. F., *The Books and the Parchments: Some Chapters on the Transmission of the Bible* (3d ed.; London: Pickering and Inglis, 1963).

*Bruce, F. F., *History of the Bible in English: From the Earliest Versions* (3d ed.; New York/London: Oxford University Press/Lutterworth Press, 1978).

Huberman, B., "Translating the Bible " in *Atlantic Monthly* 253 (1985) 43–58.

Kenyon, F., *Our Bible and the Ancient Manuscripts* (5th ed., rev. by A. W. Adams; London: Eyre and Spottiswoode, 1958).

*Kubo, S. and W. Specht, *So Many Versions? Twentieth Century English Versions of the Bible* (rev. ed.; Grand Rapids: Zondervan Publishing House, 1983).

Lewis, J. P., *The English Bible: From KJV to NIV* (Grand Rapids: Baker Book House, 1981).

Nineham, D. E. (ed.), *The New English Bible Reviewed* (London: Epworth Press, 1965).

Orlinsky, H. M., *Notes on the New Translation of the Torah* (Philadelphia: Jewish Publication Society of America, 1969).

Pope, H., *English Versions of the Bible* (rev. ed.; St. Louis/London: B. Herder, 1952).

Preliminary and Interim Report on the Hebrew Old Testament Text Project (5 vols.; ed. by the UBS committee; New York/London: United Bible Societies, 1973–1980).

Robinson, H. W., *The Bible in Its Ancient and English Versions* (London/New York: Oxford University Press, 1954).

Textual Notes on the New American Bible (Washington: Catholic Biblical Association of America, n.d.).

Weigle, L. A., *The New Testament Octapla: Eight English Versions of the New Testament in the Tyndale-King James Tradition* (New York/London: Thomas Nelson, 1962).

CHAPTER 3

HISTORICAL CRITICISM:

The Setting in Time and Space

Historical criticism of documents is based on the assumption that a text is historical in at least two senses: it may relate history as well as have its own history. For this reason, we can distinguish between the "history *in* the text" and the "history *of* the text." The former expression refers to what the text itself narrates or relates about history, whether persons, events, social conditions, or even ideas. In this sense, a text may serve as a window through which we can peer into a historical period. From a critical reading of what the text says we can draw conclusions about political, social, or religious conditions of the period or periods during which the text was produced. The latter expression refers to something different, for it is not concerned with what the text itself says or describes—the story it tells— but with the story of the text, or what one writer calls the "career of the text"—its own history: how, why, when, where, and in what circumstances it originated; by whom and for whom it was written, composed, edited, produced, and preserved; why it was produced and the various influences that affected its origin, formation, development, preservation, and transmission.

If one does a historical-critical analysis of *The Histories* of Herodotus (fifth century B.C.), for example, both of these aspects come into play. In investigating the historical and cultural descriptions in the work itself, the critic asks such questions as: Whose history is being described? What events are seen as important? Who and what are talked about in the text? What information and perspectives gained from sources outside Herodotus' work can be brought to bear on his work to aid in understanding? Are there special emphases of the author which dominate and color the presentation? How reliably does Herodotus describe matters and events? In addition to what Herodotus relates in *The Histories*—the history *in* the text—the critic also investigates the situation of the author himself and the context in which the history was written—the history *of* the text. Here the following types of questions are addressed: What is known biographically about the author and the place of this work in his life's activity? What cultural factors of the day may explain the production of the work? What tendencies and interests of the writer and his time influenced the work, its shape, and its contents? What objectives and goals did Herodotus have in mind for his work?

Historical criticism of the biblical writings is based on assumptions similar to those used in working with other ancient texts. The biblical critic is concerned with both the situation depicted in the text and the situation which gave birth to the text. The first of these is obviously of more relevance when the biblical books are concerned directly with historical matters, such as Genesis through 2 Kings, 1 and 2 Chronicles, Ezra, Nehemiah, the Gospels, and Acts. Even in nonhistorical books, such as Proverbs and Psalms, the cultural situations and conditions reflected in the texts are of concern to the interpreter. For all the biblical materials, the historical and cultural conditions out of which they came is of interest to the interpreter and an aid to understanding. This is the case even though interpreters frequently know nothing about the actual authors or collectors of various books.

These two aspects of historical criticism were applied in a limited fashion to biblical writings by ancient Jewish and Christian interpreters as well as by others. Jewish interpreters tried to assign the various Old Testament books to particular authors and even debated such issues as whether Moses could have written the account of his own death found in Deuteronomy 34. Tradition sought, for example, to depict the life situation within which David supposedly wrote many of the Psalms, and this appears even in the biblical text itself (see Psalms 3; 7; 18; 34; 51; 52; 54; 56; 57; 59; 60; 63; and 142). Such matters as chronological problems and discrepancies in the text were also recognized. The Christian, Julius Africanus (d. 245), produced a world history and major encyclopedia and analyzed some biblical texts with regard to their historical reliability. Jerome (d. 420) reports that he once received a letter from a lady inquiring about the discrepancies in the Gospel accounts of Jesus' resurrection and appearances. Two pagan writers, Celsus (second century A.D.) and Porphyry (d. 303), wrote volumes in which they addressed both of these historical dimensions. They not only challenged the reliability of what was reported in some texts on the basis of internal evidence but also challenged what was taught about some texts, for example, the traditional authorship of some books.

Ancient interpreters, however, sought to defend both what was written in and what was reported about the text by attempting to resolve problems within the text and by defending traditional views about authorship. One way in which they did this was to attempt, at all costs, to harmonize discrepancies in the text. A rabbinic axiom held that in Scripture "there is no before nor after," that is, chronological problems must be ignored or overcome.

Little did ancient Jewish and Christian interpreters recognize that discrepancies in the text might be the result of two different texts having been woven or edited together, each reflecting a different viewpoint or stemming from a different historical setting. Nor was there a clear recognition that two conflicting texts, perhaps from different books, might stem from different historical periods, with one reflecting an earlier, the other a later outlook. We might say that ancient interpreters overlooked, minimized, or ignored the history *of* the text and tended to read the Bible "on the flat." Exegesis based on such a view of the text failed to appreciate that the Bible is an anthology of writings, deriving from different historical contexts and cultural situations, produced and collected over centuries.

Since the development of modern historical consciousness and the resulting methodologies which this has produced, the historical aspects of the biblical materials have received greater attention in exegesis and can really no longer be respectfully ignored. Instead we must ask: How does the exegete utilize and benefit from historical criticism? What are the tools that can be used to facilitate this endeavor?

We shall deal first with matters pertaining to the history *in* the text, or the situation the text describes. Quite obviously, if the text contains references to persons, places, and customs strange to the reader, it will be necessary to become acquainted sufficiently with the historical period or cultural setting described in the text to understand what is being said at the most elementary level. The tools most useful for obtaining this type of information will normally be the standard Bible dictionaries and encyclopedias. Equally useful, however, will be histories, sociological descriptions, and handbooks of the period being described. Histories of Israel and of early Christianity are the most useful sources to consult on matters of history, chronology, names, and events. In addition to these, individual books on the culture, sociological context, and social life of biblical times may provide well-organized information on different facets of daily life presupposed or referred to by the text. This type of information is quite often included in Bible atlases and geographies, but obviously these will be most valuable in locating place names and other geographical information pertinent to understanding the text.

Another source that can often illuminate the situation depicted in the text itself is comparative non-biblical literature. Other writings of antiquity may reflect a similar outlook, derive from roughly the same period, discuss the same topic, or provide valuable background information. The importance of these parallel references has been recognized for centuries, but they have received even greater prominence since the beginning of the twentieth century, often by scholars interested in studying the history of ancient religious traditions other than Judaism and early Christianity. This "history-of-religions" approach uncovered and collected vast amounts of materials from the ancient world which have shed light and provided new insights on the biblical writings. For example, by reading the creation stories of Genesis 1—3 alongside other creation stories from the ancient Near Eastern world, we can note both similarities and differences and understand the biblical texts even better. Similarly, archaeological discoveries have unearthed hundreds of letters and other ordinary documents from daily life especially from the Hellenistic-Roman period. Comparison of these with New Testament letters has greatly contributed to our understanding of both the form and content of the latter. Historical scholarship in the last two centuries has profoundly affected every aspect of our biblical understanding. Not only has our understanding of particular passages been increased, but also our knowledge of the history and language of the biblical text itself. This has led to an increased awareness that the biblical writings reflect the historical situation out of which they arose. Recognizing this historical dimension of biblical writings is now regarded as an essential feature of any informed exegesis of a biblical text. For this reason, most biblical commentaries, especially those produced within the past century, provide numerous references to such parallel texts and normally incorporate insights gained from studying such documents into the interpretation provided of the text itself.

In order to locate such parallel texts, the student should consult two kinds of sources: (a) critical commentaries, which usually provide references in footnotes and (b) anthologies of writings from the ancient world, usually arranged by literary genre, such as "creation stories," "legal texts," "historical documents," "birth stories," "letters," "apocalypses," and so forth.

The second historical dimension the exegete should explore is the history *of* the text, or the situation out of which the text arose—the situation of the author and the audience. It is now well-known that many of the biblical books are anonymous, even though later tradition assigned authors to them. None of the four Gospels, for example, contains an explicit reference to who wrote them, even though in the second and third centuries they were assigned to Matthew, Mark, Luke, and John. In fact, it is now widely recognized that many of the writings of the Bible were edited rather than written by single individuals and that many persons and groups engaged in this editing process which, in some instances, extended over a period of decades or even centuries. Especially is this the case with the Pentateuch, but also with other parts of the Bible as well. This has required a shift in the way in which interpreters understand the relationship between the biblical writings and the original senders and receivers of these writings. In very few instances does it appear that a single author penned a writing, from start to finish, in one sitting. Even in those cases where this appears to have happened, there is strong evidence suggesting that these writings frequently continued to be edited, either by the author, or by the author's successors.

In some instances, the situation described in the text and the situation out of which the text arose may reflect the same historical setting. On the other hand, these two situations may represent different historical settings, separated by long periods of time. The situation described in Paul's letters to the Corinthians is contemporary with Paul's own situation. Handbooks describing the mid-fifties of the first century A.D. will be useful in illuminating both. The Pentateuch, on the other hand, was obviously written much later than the events which it purports to describe. Similarily, the Gospels were written considerably later than the events they describe. In such cases, the exegete should seek to determine as much as possible about the situation out of which the passage or its source arose, as well as the historical situation it describes.

One of the best illustrations of this point occurs in the Old Testament book of Daniel, where the events depicted in the text extend from the sixth to the second century but the time of the book's final composition has been established as the mid-second century B.C. To understand a passage from the book of Daniel, therefore, will require the interpreter to become familiar both with the sixth century, the period it describes, and the second century, the period in which it was written. Similarly, in interpreting the Gospels, it may be important to know about historical developments in Judaism and Christianity within the last quarter of the first century A.D., the time of their probable composition, as it is the first thirty years of the first century, the time of Jesus' ministry. For example, to understand Jesus' polemic against the Pharisees in Matthew 23, it is as important to know the history of Jewish-Christian relations after A.D. 70 as it is to know the history of Pharisaism in the time of Jesus.

Obviously, an important part of the history *of* the text is the author of the text, and this introduces two further considerations: (a) the issue of multiple authorship of a text and (b) the problem of pseudonymous authorship of a text. These may be considered in turn.

Although we often find a passage within a biblical book under the title of a single author, such as Isaiah, Solomon, Matthew, or Paul, we cannot assume necessarily in an exegesis of the passage that it contains the words of such an individual in an unqualified sense. We may in fact discover that it is impossible to determine who actually wrote the text or who actually is responsible for the final form of the text, and that the interpretation of the passage will have to be modified accordingly. As we noted earlier, exegesis often requires the interpreter to be far more modest in what can be asserted about the text than the pre-understanding assumed at the outset. The standard handbooks on the Old Testament provide detailed descriptions of the most well-known instance of this, namely, the multiple authorship of the Pentateuch and the various historical contexts in which its different parts arose. We noted earlier the common practice in antiquity of collecting writings under the name of a revered individual of the past or of assigning writings to such an individual. Apocalyptic writing, such as the book of Daniel mentioned above, provides numerous instances of this, but it also occurs elsewhere in the biblical writings. The canonical book of Isaiah, though constituting a single book within the Old Testament, is now widely recognized as the work of at least two separate "authors," one addressing an eighth-century B.C. situation, the other a sixth century B.C. situation. In the New Testament, thirteen writings are attributed to the Apostle Paul and yet his authorship of six of these is widely disputed. They may have been compiled and collected into their final form after Paul's death, although still attributed to him.

Such questions of authorship and context are dealt with extensively in introductions to the Old and New Testaments, as well as in the introductory sections of commentaries on biblical books. On any particular passage, the student may check either of these sources for help in determining whether the passage is assumed to be the result of pseudonymous or multiple authorship and whether it reflects a period of time much later than that described in the passage itself.

Yet another aspect of this "external history" involves the literary composition of the text itself. This will be treated much more fully in a later chapter on literary criticism but it deserves to be mentioned here because it too is part of the history *of* the text. Because the final form of the biblical text has often been the result of extensive editing, a single book may contain units whose relationship to each other is not altogether clear. Such sections may have been inserted, or interpolated, into the writing, and the interpreter will need to determine, if possible, why this was done and how. For example, many of the prophetic books of the Old Testament are not uniform literary compositions, but contain sections consisting of narratives and oracles whose relationship to each other may be unclear. Some of the Pauline letters are actually composite documents where smaller letters or fragments of letters have been combined into a single document. In such cases, the interpreter cannot assume that the same historical setting gave rise to all the documents but instead must be open to a variety of possibilities.

A third aspect of the external history of a passage may be mentioned. This has to do with the way in which certain parts of the Biblc have incorporated older biblical traditions and reinterpreted them by presenting them in a new, modified form. The Old Testament books of Chronicles are best understood as re-presentations of the books of Kings but written from a different standpoint. Similarly, in the book of Daniel we find that older biblical traditions have been appropriated and reinterpreted. In chapter 9, the interpretation of the seventy years of desolation draws on Jeremiah (25:11–12; 29:10) which itself is based on an ancient Near Eastern formulaic tradition. In the New Testament, Matthew and Luke are probably directly dependent on Mark, yet they have expanded Mark's story considerably and altered it in many respects.

This reminds the interpreter that much of the biblical material is genetically related in the sense that earlier materials are taken up, incorporated, and re-presented in later materials. Viewed this way, the biblical materials themselves are seen to have undergone historical development, and this forms a valuable perspective for the interpreter. For example, if we are interpreting a passage in Matthew, we should be aware that it stands further along the historical continuum than Mark and that even if the same event is being reported in both Gospels, the "situation of the author" might be radically different in each case, different enough, perhaps, to provide a different understanding of both texts.

This becomes especially important as we attempt to interpret both the Old and New Testaments together, for the latter presupposes the former, and in many cases cites it directly. In trying to understand a New Testament passage in which the Old Testament is cited or referred to, we may greatly benefit by realizing that this Old Testament passage has been interpreted and reinterpreted many times between the period of its original composition and its incorporation into the New Testament text. A New Testament text must frequently be understood in light of the history of interpretation of an Old Testament text.

This may be stated another way. The authors of the biblical writings were not only composing new texts, but also often transmitting and interpreting older texts and traditions as well. Seen this way, much of the Bible may be said to have originated as a series of interpretations in which authors took older traditions and reinterpreted them in light of their own situation. Nor did this chain of interpretation cease when the biblical writings ceased to be written or even when the biblical documents were collected into their final canonical form. Long after the Old and New Testament writings were recognized as canonical, Jewish and Christian authors continued to quote and interpret them, and their interpretations can be extremely illuminating to the contemporary interpreter as well. By paying attention to this "historical foreground," as well as to the "historical background" of the biblical documents, we can often see a passage of Scripture in a new light and develop new levels of understanding which would otherwise be missed by trying to make the theoretical jump from the twentieth century to the first century or earlier.

To cite a specific example, we may refer to the well-known reference to a "virgin's" conceiving a child, first mentioned in Isaiah 7:14 and later quoted in both Matthew and Luke. If the student is interpreting Matthew 1:21, it must be recognized that the passage may not mean the same in the context of Isaiah as in the context of Matthew since the passage itself has its own history of interpretation. It will be necessary to examine the passage in its Isaiah setting, trace the ways it was used and interpreted in the centuries prior to the Christian era, and also to examine the different ways it is interpreted in the New Testament writings. Having done so, it will then be useful to see how later Christian writers understood the same passage. We can thus easily see that because the "historical career" of a text may be long and continuous, it may provide us a useful perspective by which we can develop our own interpretation of the passage.

BIBLIOGRAPHY

Dictionaries and Encyclopedias

*Achtemeier, P. J. (ed.), *Harper's Bible Dictionary* (San Francisco/London: Harper & Row, 1985).

Bromiley, G. W. (ed.), *International Standard Bible Encyclopedia* (rev. ed.; 4 vols.; Grand Rapids: Eerdmans Publishing Company, 1979–).

*Buttrick, G. A. (ed.), *Interpreter's Dictionary of the Bible* (4 vols.; Nashville: Abingdon Press, 1962; *Supplementary Volume*, ed. by K. Crim, 1976).

Douglas, J. D. et al. (eds.), *The New Bible Dictionary* (Leicester/Grand Rapids: Inter-Varsity Press/Eerdmans Publishing Company, 1962).

Encyclopaedia Judaica (16 vols.: Jerusalem/New York: Keter Publishing House Ltd./Macmillan, 1971).

Gehman, H. S. (ed.), *The New Westminster Dictionary of the Bible* (Philadelphia: Westminster Press, 1970).

Hastings, J. (ed.), *Dictionary of the Bible* (rev. ed. by F. C. Grant and H. H. Rowley; Edinburgh/New York: T. & T. Clark/Charles Scribner's Sons, 1963).

McKenzie, J. L., *Dictionary of the Bible* (Milwaukee/London: Bruce Publishing Company/Geoffrey Chapman, 1966).

Histories of Israel and Judah

Bright, J., *A History of Israel* (3d ed.; Philadelphia/London: Westminster Press/ SCM Press, 1981).

Castel, F., *The History of Israel and Judah in Old Testament Times* (Mahwah, NJ: Paulist Press, 1983).

Hayes, J. H. and J. M. Miller (eds.), *Israelite and Judaean History* (Philadelphia/London: Westminster Press/SCM Press, 1977).

Herrmann, S., *A History of Israel in Old Testament Times* (2d ed.; London/Philadelphia: SCM Press/Fortress Press, 1981).

Jagersma, H., *A History of Israel in the Old Testament Period* (London/Philadelphia: SCM Press/Fortress Press, 1982).

*Miller, J. M. and J. H. Hayes, *A History of Ancient Israel and Judah* (Philadelphia/London: Westminster Press/SCM Press, 1986).

Noth, M., *The History of Israel* (2d ed.; London/New York: A. & C. Black/ Harper & Row, 1960).

Soggin, J. A., *A History of Israel: From the Beginnings to the Bar Kochba Revolt, AD 135* (London/Philadelphia: SCM Press/Westminster Press, 1984/ 1985).

de Vaux, R., *The Early History of Israel* (London/Philadelphia: Darton, Longman, and Todd/Westminster Press, 1978).

World History of the Jewish People: Ancient Times (Tel Aviv/Jerusalem: Massada Publishing Co., 1964–).

History and Literature of Intertestamental Judaism

*Cohen, S. J. D., *From the Maccabees to the Mishnah* (Philadelphia/London: Westminster Press/SPCK, 1987).

Collins, J. J., *Between Athens and Jerusalem: Jewish Identity in the Hellenistic Diaspora* (New York: Crossroad, 1982).

Hengel, M., *Judaism and Hellenism: Studies in Their Encounter in Palestine During the Early Hellenistic Period* (2 vols.; London/Philadelphia: SCM Press/Fortress Press, 1974).

Mulder, M. J. et al. (eds.), *The Literature of the Jewish People in the Period of the Second Temple and Talmud* (3 vols.; Assen/Philadelphia: Van Gorcum/ Fortress Press, 1984–).

*Nickelsburg, G. W. E., *Jewish Literature Between the Bible and the Mishnah: A Historical and Literary Introduction* (Philadelphia/London: Fortress Press/ SCM Press, 1981).

*Schürer, E., *The History of the Jewish People in the Age of Jesus Christ* (175 BC—AD *135): A New English Version Revised and Edited* (ed. by G. Vermes and F. Millar et al.; 3 vols.; Edinburgh: T. & T. Clark, 1973–).

Histories of Early Christianity

Bruce, F. F., *New Testament History* (London/Garden City: Oliphants/Double-day & Company, 1969/1972).

*Conzelmann, H., *History of Primitive Christianity* (Nashville: Abingdon Press, 1973).

Filson, F. V., *A New Testament History: The Story of the Emerging Church* (London/Philadelphia: SCM Press/Westminster Press, 1964).

Goppelt, L., *Apostolic and Post-Apostolic Times* (London: A. & C. Black, 1970; reprinted, Grand Rapids: Baker Book House, 1977).

*Leaney, A. R. C., *The Jewish and Christian World 200 BC to AD 200* (Cambridge/New York: Cambridge University Press, 1985).

Lietzmann, H., *A History of the Early Church* (4 vols.; London: Lutterworth Press, 1937–1951; reprinted in 2 vols.; Cleveland/New York: World Publishing Co., 1961).

Pfeiffer, R. H., *History of New Testament Times with an Introduction to the Apocrypha* (New York: Harper & Brothers, 1949).

Reicke, B., *The New Testament Era: The World of the Bible from 500 BC to AD 100* (Philadelphia/London: Fortress Press/A. & C. Black, 1968/1969).

Weiss, J., *Earliest Christianity: A History of the Period AD 30–150* (2 vols.; New York: Wilson-Erickson 1937; reissued, Gloucester: Peter Smith, 1970).

Atlases and Geographies

Aharoni, Y., *The Land of the Bible: A Historical Geography* (rev. ed. by A. F. Rainey; Philadelphia/London: Westminster Press/Burns & Oates, 1979/1980).

*Aharoni, Y. and M. Avi-Yonah, *The Macmillan Bible Atlas* (rev. ed.; New York/London: Macmillan Publishing Company/Collier Macmillan Company, 1977).

Avi-Yonah, M., *The Holy Land from the Persian to the Arab Conquests (536 BC to AD 640): A Historical Geography* (rev. ed.; Grand Rapids: Baker Book House, 1977).

Baly, D., *Geographical Companion to the Bible* (New York/London: McGraw-Hill/Lutterworth Press, 1963).

Baly, D., *The Geography of the Bible* (2d ed.; New York/London: Harper & Row/Lutterworth Press, 1979).

Grollenberg, L. H., *Atlas of the Bible* (London/New York: Thomas Nelson, 1956).

Grollenberg, L. H., *The Penguin Shorter Atlas of the Bible* (Harmondsworth/ Baltimore: Penguin Books, 1978).

*May, H. G., *Oxford Bible Atlas* (3d ed.; rev. by J. Day; New York/London: Oxford University Press, 1984).

Rogerson, J., *Atlas of the Bible* (London/New York: Facts on File, 1984).

*Smith, G. A., *Historical Geography of the Holy Land* (4th ed.; London: Hodder and Stoughton, 1896; reprinted by various publishers).

Wright, G. E. and F. V. Filson, *The Westminster Historical Atlas to the Bible* (rev. ed.; Philadelphia: Westminster Press, 1956).

Archaeology

Aharoni, Y., *The Archaeology of the Land of Israel* (Philadelphia/London: Westminster Press/SCM Press, 1982).

Albright, W. F., *The Archaeology of Palestine* (new ed., rev. by W. G. Dever; Gloucester: Peter Smith, 1976).

*Avi-Yonah, M. (ed.), *Encyclopedia of Archaeological Excavations in the Holy Land* (4 vols.; London/Englewood Cliffs: Oxford University Press/Prentice-Hall, 1976–1979).

Blaiklock, E. M. and R. K. Harrison (eds.), *The New International Dictionary of Biblical Archaeology* (Grand Rapids: Zondervan Publishing House, 1984).

Finegan, J., *Archaeological History of the Ancient Middle East* (Boulder/Folkestone: Westview Press/Dawson & Sons Ltd., 1979).

Finegan, J., *The Archaeology of the New Testament: The Life of Jesus and the Beginning of the Early Church* (Princeton: Princeton University Press, 1969).

Finegan, J., *The Archaeology of the New Testament: The Mediterranean World of the Early Christian Apostles* (Boulder/Beckenham/Croom Helm: Westview Press, 1981).

Kenyon, K. M., *Archaeology in the Holy Land* (4th ed.; London/New York: Ernest Benn Limited/W. W. Norton and Company, 1974).

Kenyon, K. M., *The Bible and Recent Archaeology* (London/Atlanta: British Museum/John Knox Press, 1978).

Lance, H. D., *The Old Testament and the Archaeologist* (Philadelphia/London: Fortress Press/SPCK, 1981).

Schoville, K. N., *Biblical Archaeology in Focus* (Grand Rapids: Baker Book House, 1978).

Thomas, D. N., *Archaeology and Old Testament Study* (London/New York: Oxford University Press, 1967).

Thompson, J. A., *The Bible and Archaeology* (2d ed.; Grand Rapids/Exeter: Eerdmans Publishing Company/Paternoster Press, 1972/1973).

Wright, G. E., *Biblical Archaeology* (rev. ed.: Philadelphia/London: Westminster Press/Gerald Duckworth & Co., Ltd.; 1962).

Biblical Backgrounds: Culture and Daily Life

Aune, D. E., *The New Testament in Its Literary Environment* (Philadelphia/ London: Westminster Press/SPCK, 1987).

Bickerman, E. J., *Chronology of the Ancient World* (London/Ithaca: Thames and Hudson/Cornell University Press, 1968).

Bouquet, A. C., *Everyday Life in New Testament Times* (London/New York: B. T. Batsford/Charles Scribner's Sons, 1953).

Cary, M. and T. J. Haarhoff, *Life and Thought in the Greek and Roman World* (London/New York: Methuen/Barnes and Noble, 1940).

Finegan, J., *Handbook of Biblical Chronology: Principles of Time Reckoning in the Ancient World and Problems of Chronology in the Bible* (Princeton: Princeton University Press, 1964).

Gager, J. G., *Kingdom and Community: The Social World of Early Christianity* (Englewood Cliffs/Hempstead: Prentice-Hall, 1975).

Harrison, R. K., *Old Testament Times* (Grand Rapids/Leicester: Eerdmans Publishing Company/Inter-Varsity Press, 1970/1972).

Heaton, E. W., *Everyday Life in Old Testament Times* (London/New York: B. T. Batsford/Charles Scribner's Sons, 1956).

Jeremias, J., *Jerusalem in the Time of Jesus: An Investigation into Economic and Social Conditions During the New Testament Period* (Philadelphia/ London: Fortress Press/SCM Press, 1969).

*Koester, H., *Introduction to the New Testament*, vol. 1: *History, Culture, and Religion of the Hellenistic Age* (Philadelphia: Fortress Press, 1982).

*Lohse, E., *The New Testament Environment* (Nashville/London: Abingdon Press/SCM Press, 1976).

Malina, B. J., *The New Testament World: Insights from Cultural Anthropology* (Atlanta: John Knox Press, 1981).

Malina, B. J., *Christian Origins and Cultural Anthropology* (Atlanta: John Knox Press, 1986).

Malherbe, A. J., *Social Aspects of Early Christianity* (2d ed.; Philadelphia: Fortress Press, 1983).

Meeks, W. A., *The First Urban Christians: The Social World of the Apostle Paul* (New Haven/London: Yale University Press, 1983).

Meeks, W. A., *The Moral World of the First Christians* (Philadelphia/London: Westminster Press/SPCK, 1987).

*Noth, M., *The Old Testament World* (London/Philadelphia: A. & C. Black/ Fortress Press, 1966).

*Roetzel, C. J., *The World That Shaped the New Testament* (Atlanta/London: John Knox Press/SCM Press, 1985/1987).

Safrai, S. and M. Stern (eds.), *The Jewish People in the First Christian Century* (2 vols.; Assen/Philadelphia: Van Gorcum/Fortress Press, 1974–1976).

Stambaugh, J. E. and D. L. Balch, *The New Testament in Its Social Environment* (Philadephia/London: Westminster Press/SPCK, 1986).

Theissen, G., *The First Followers of Jesus: A Sociological Analysis of the Earliest Christianity/Sociology of Early Palestinian Christianity* (London/Philadelphia: SCM Press/Fortress Press, 1978).

Theissen, G., *The Social Setting of Pauline Christianity* (Edinburgh/Philadelphia: T. & T. Clark/Fortress Press, 1982).

de Vaux, R., *Ancient Israel: Its Life and Institutions* (New York/London: McGraw-Hill/Darton, Longman and Todd, 1961).

Wilson, R. R., *Sociological Approaches to the Old Testament* (Philadelphia: Fortress Press, 1984).

Wiseman, D. J. (ed.), *Peoples of Old Testament Times* (London/New York: Oxford University Press, 1973).

*van der Woude, A. S. (ed.), *The World of the Bible* (Grand Rapids: Eerdmans Publishing Company, 1986).

Collections of Non-Biblical Comparative Materials

Barnstone, W. (ed.), *The Other Bible: Ancient Esoteric Texts from the Pseudepigrapha, the Dead Sea Scrolls, the Nag Hammadi Library, and Other Sources* (San Francisco: Harper & Row, 1984).

Barrett, C. K., *The New Testament Background: Selected Documents* (London/New York: SPCK/Harper & Row, 1956).

Beyerlin, W. (ed.), *Near Eastern Religious Texts Relating to the Old Testament* (London/Philadelphia: SCM Press/Westminster Press, 1978).

Cartlidge, D.R. and D. L. Dungan, *Documents for the Study of the Gospels: A Sourcebook for the Comparative Study of the Gospels* (London/Philadelphia: Collins Liturgical Publications/Fortress Press, 1980).

Charlesworth, J. H., *The Old Testament Pseudepigrapha* (2 vols.; Garden City/London: Doubleday & Company/Darton, Longman and Todd, 1983-1985).

Crossan, J. D., *Sayings Parallels: A Workbook for the Jesus Tradition* (Philadelphia/London: Fortress Press/SCM Press, 1986).

Hennecke, E. and W. Schneemelcher (eds.), *New Testament Apocrypha* (2 vols.; London/Philadelphia: Lutterworth Press/Westminster Press, 1963–1965).

Kee, H. C., *The Origins of Christianity: Sources and Documents* (Englewood Cliffs/London: Prentice-Hall/SPCK, 1973).

Malherbe, A. J., *Moral Exhortation: A Greco-Roman Sourcebook* (Philadelphia/London: Westminster Press/SCM Press, 1986).

Montefiore, C. G. and H. Loewe, *A Rabbinic Anthology* (New York: Schocken Books, 1974).

Nickelsburg, G. W. E. and M. E. Stone, *Faith and Piety in Early Judaism: Texts and Documents* (Philadelphia: Fortress Press, 1983).

Pritchard, J. B., *The Ancient Near East in Pictures Relating to the Old Testament* (2d ed.; Princeton: Princeton University Press, 1969).

*Pritchard, J. B., (ed.), *Ancient Near Eastern Texts Relating to the Old Testament* (3d ed.; Princeton: Princeton University Press, 1969).

Robinson, J. M. (ed.), *The Nag Hammadi Library in English* (San Francisco: Harper & Row, 1977).

*Sparks, H. F. D. (ed.), *The Apocryphal Old Testament* (London/New York: Oxford University Press, 1984).

Thomas, D. W. (ed.), *Documents from Old Testament Times* (London/New York: Thomas Nelson & Sons, Ltd./Harper Torchbooks, 1958/1961).

Vermes, G., *The Dead Sea Scrolls in English* (2d ed.; Hammondsworth/Baltimore: Penguin Books, 1975).

*Whittaker, M., *Jews and Christians: Graeco-Roman Views* (Cambridge/New York: Cambridge University Press, 1985).

Introductions to the Old Testament

Childs, B. S., *Introduction to the Old Testament as Scripture* (London/Philadelphia: SCM Press/Fortress Press, 1979).

*Eissfeldt, O., *The Old Testament: An Introduction Including the Apocrypha and Pseudepigrapha and Also the Works of a Similar Type from Qumran* (Oxford/New York: Basil Blackwell/Harper & Row, 1965).

Fohrer, G., *Introduction to the Old Testament* (Nashville/London: Abingdon Press/SPCK, 1968).

Gottwald, N. K., *The Hebrew Bible—A Socioliterary Introduction* (Philadelphia/London: Fortress Press/SCM Press, 1985).

Harrison, R. K., *Introduction to the Old Testament: With a Comprehensive Review of Old Testament Studies and a Special Supplement on the Apocrypha* (Leicester/Grand Rapids: Inter-Varsity Press/Eerdmans Publishing Company, 1969).

*Hayes, J. H., *Introduction to Old Testament Study* (Nashville/London: Abingdon Press/SCM Press, 1979/1982).

Kaiser, O., *Introduction to the Old Testament* (Oxford/Minneapolis: Blackwell/Augsburg, 1980).

Rendtorff, R., *The Old Testament: An Introduction* (London/Philadelphia: SCM Press/Fortress Press, 1985).

Schmidt, W. H., *Old Testament Introduction* (New York/London: Crossroad/SCM Press, 1984).

Soggin, J. A., *Introduction to the Old Testament: From Its Origins to the Closing of the Alexandrian Canon* (rev. ed.; London/Philadelphia: SCM Press/Westminster Press, 1980).

Introductions to the New Testament

Childs, B. S., *The New Testament as Canon: An Introduction* (London/Philadelphia: SCM Press/Fortress Press, 1984/1985).

Guthrie, D., *New Testament Introduction* (3d ed.; London/Downers Grove: Tyndale Press/Inter-Varsity Press, 1970/1971).

*Johnson, L. T., *The Writings of the New Testament: An Interpretation* (Philadelphia/London: Fortress Press/SCM Press, 1986).

Koester, H., *Introduction to the New Testament* (2 vols.; Philadelphia; Fortress Press, 1982).

Kümmel, W. G., *Introduction to the New Testament* (rev. ed.; Nashville/London: Abingdon Press/SCM Press, 1975/1977).

Marxsen, W., *Introduction to the New Testament: An Approach to Its Problems* (Philadelphia/Oxford: Fortress Press/Basil Blackwell, 1968).

Perrin, N. and D. C. Duling, *The New Testament, An Introduction: Proclamation and Parenesis, Myth and History* (2d ed.; New York/London: Harcourt Brace Jovanovich, 1982).

Wikenhauser, A., *New Testament Introduction* (Dublin/New York: Herder and Herder, 1958).

CHAPTER 4

GRAMMATICAL CRITICISM:

The Language of the Text

If textual criticism is concerned with establishing the wording of the text, and historical criticism with investigating the history *in* and *of* the text, grammatical criticism is concerned with analyzing a text through its language. To be sure, language consists of words, but ideas and concepts rather than being conveyed through words standing alone are transmitted through words arranged in various combinations with each other. Grammatical criticism is concerned not only with how individual words function as carriers of meaning but how those words are arranged in phrases and sentences to form meaningful sense units. This type of criticism may be thought of as the set of skills and disciplines through which we seek to re-create and enter the original thought world of the author (or text) through the language of the text.

We may begin by looking at the way in which we analyze the most fundamental unit of communication—the word. Even though we recognize that the message of a text is not conveyed in and through single words standing alone but rather through phrases and sentences arranged in sense units, we must nonetheless deal with single words and phrases. One reason for this is that when we read a text, we often meet words or phrases whose reference or meaning we as twentieth-century readers find unfamiliar, if not unintelligible. This is especially the case with terms that were used in special ways or with special senses in the communities of Israel and the early church, or whose ancient usage differs significantly from their modern usage.

While certain words and phrases, such as the names of persons and places, will be investigated as part of historical criticism, others will not. Such terms as "remnant," "covenant," "repentance,"or "justification" receive special treatment in Bible dictionaries and encyclopedias because of their historical context and their significance in the Bible. For this reason, definitions of such terms in standard English dictionaries will be adequate only at the most elementary level and may actually turn out to be unsatisfactory, given their brevity and English-language perspective.

Quite often, we can begin our analysis of the text by isolating prominent words or expressions that we suspect are important but whose meaning we may find unclear. For example, in Jeremiah 31:31–34, the well-known passage proclaiming the coming of a "new covenant," we immediately recognize that the term "covenant" is so central to the passage that we must investigate it thoroughly in order to understand the passage. By concentrating on this single term and its frequent uses throughout the Bible, we can learn more about the Israelite understanding of "covenant." As we do so, other aspects of the passage will come into much sharper focus. Or, if we are exegeting Matthew 16:29, where Jesus asserts that some of those in his audience would not die before they saw "the Son of man coming in his kingdom," we can easily see that the phrases "Son of man" and "kingdom" will need to be investigated thoroughly before we can understand the passage. Again, by concentrating on these single expressions, we can investigate how they are used and what they denote in the Gospel of Matthew, in other New Testament writings, as well as in other writings of the first century A.D. As we learn more about first-century usage of these expressions, we are better able to make sense of their use in Matthew 16:29.

In dealing with individual words or phrases, three kinds of exegetical tools are invaluable. The first of these are Bible dictionaries and encyclopedias. These contain articles treating important biblical ideas and concepts, and such articles are usually comprehensive in nature, yet sufficiently specific to provide the exegete with a general grasp of the issues. They will also provide useful bibliography for further study.

A second type of resource whose focus is more narrow and thus gives more specific information is biblical wordbooks and lexicons. These are more oriented toward providing information about the language itself than about biblical history and culture per se. Single-volume wordbooks contain useful word studies of important biblical terms as well as broader concepts to which a whole cluster of biblical terms may relate. Multivolume wordbooks are available on both the Old and New Testaments, and although based on the original languages, they are quite useful to students who know neither Hebrew nor Greek. These contain extensive articles on individual words, arranged in word families, in which the usage of terms is treated historically, from the time of their earliest usage until the time of their occurrence in the biblical texts, and even after. Though these articles are designed to provide philological and linguistic information, they are nevertheless a mine of theological, historical, cultural, and bibliographical information as well.

A third source for investigating the language of the text is the biblical concordance. As is well known, the concordance provides little or no explanatory information comparable to that found in a Bible dictionary, encyclopedia, wordbook, or lexicon. Its primary purpose is to list the various biblical verses in which a word occurs. Ordinarily, the line of the passage in which the word or phrase occurs is given to assist the reader in discerning the context. For this reason, perhaps the most frequent use of this tool is to assist us in locating a verse in the Bible when we can remember only a word or phrase from the verse. As valuable as this may be, we can make far more sophisticated use of the concordance than this. In fact, when properly used, it may well become the single most useful tool at the exegete's disposal.

We should begin by recognizing that there are various types of concordances. First, some concordances (such as Cruden, *Nelson's Complete Concordance of the RSV*) simply list all the words of the Bible in alphabetical order and under each word the biblical passages in which the word occurs arranged in canonical order. If, for example, we want to know all the places in the Bible where the word "covenant" occurs, rather than having to read through the entire Bible, find them on our own, and list them by hand, we can simply turn in the concordance to "covenant" and find that this basic work of collection has already been done for us. In this type of concordance, however, all the passages from Genesis through Revelation are listed with no attempt made to differentiate or classify the various meanings or usages of the word.

Second, some concordances are "analytical." They classify all the passages in which a term occurs into sub-categories based on (a) the different Hebrew or Greek words that are translated by a single English word, (b) general themes or topics under which several different words may be included, and (c) the different senses or uses of a single word or expression. We may look at these in turn.

(a) The first type of analytical concordance (such as Young, Strong, and Morrison) enables the exegete to determine which Hebrew or Greek word the English term translates. This becomes a useful step for doing further word study, and a necessary one if we want to use the various tools that are based on the original language.

(b) The second type of analytical concordance (such as Darton) takes seriously the fact that several different words may all relate to the same theme or topic, and are thus best dealt with as a single group. Since this type of concordance is more thematic in its organization, it can be quite useful in investigating broader concepts or topics that may encompass several different biblical words.

(c) A third type of analytical concordance (such as Lisowsky, Moulton and Geden, and Aland) employs a principle of classification which recognizes that even the same Hebrew or Greek word or expression may be used in various senses throughout the biblical writings. Accordingly, it groups together all those passages in which a term is used in a similar sense. This may be shown by key indicators listed at the beginning of the entry or by arranging the passages in separate groups. In either case, this type of arrangement greatly assists the exegete because it provides a natural place to begin the investigation without having to examine every single biblical verse in which the word occurs.

As we noted earlier, comparative non-biblical literature can be quite illuminating for understanding the meaning and use of biblical terminology. Where concordances exist for this literature (such as the *Concordance to the Apocrypha/Deuterocanonical Books of the RSV* and Hatch and Redpath, which includes the apocryphal writings), the same process of investigation can be pursued in these writings. Frequently, a broad investigation of a term's usage can reveal diverse information which may be relevant to our understanding of its usage in a particular text or author.

Once we have looked up an important term in the concordance, located the relevant passages where it occurs, we can then develop interpretive questions with which to explore the material: Does the term appear to be used in the same sense in the different passages? Does it have a technical meaning? Do there appear to be different nuances in its various usages? If so, why? In what type of literature does the term occur? Is it always used in the same type of literature or the same historical setting? Does it have a literal or metaphorical meaning? Does it tend to be used by one author or in one section of biblical writings to the exclusion of others? If so, why? Does this provide a clue to understanding an individual verse or section or even a writing as a whole?

By asking questions such as these—and many others that occur to us as we work with the material—we gradually broaden our understanding of the term, the passage itself and the other biblical writings in which it occurs. It is through this process of interrogation and analysis that we begin to increase our own understanding of the passage by actually re-entering and re-creating the thought-world of the author or text itself.

We can see how this is done by looking at the example we mentioned earlier, the use of Son of man in Matthew 16:29. If we look up this expression in an analytical concordance (such as Young, Strong, or Moulton and Geden), we immediately notice several things. First, the term tends to cluster in certain biblical writings. It is used most frequently in the New Testament, and there primarily in the Synoptic Gospels. To begin with, we might note that the term is relatively unimportant, or even inconsequential, in the Pauline and Johannine writings. This negative observation can be useful because it provides a point of contrast with the Matthean usage. Second, the term occurs in the Old Testament in several places, and in several senses. Here, we should note these different senses (which are already classified for us in an analytical concordance) and ask which of these, if any, bear on the usage in our passage. As it turns out, a crucial exegetical question discussed in commentaries is whether the term used by Jesus in the Gospels has a general sense as it does in Ezekiel, or a more technical sense as it does in Daniel. Third, if we examine the usages of the term in Matthew alone, we discover that it is used in at least three ways: (a) in a general sense, almost as a synonymn for "man" or "human being," (b) in an eschatological sense to refer to a figure who will appear at the end of time as judge, and (c) in a specifically christological sense, especially when the suffering of the Messiah is discussed. Our task, at this point, is to determine in which of these senses it is used in Matthew 16:29 and to relate it to the other two. From here, it is a natural move to make a similar investigation of the term in Mark and Luke, trying to determine how they are related to Matthew, if at all. Fourth, we could expand our investigation by examining the use of the term in non-biblical writings, especially the Old Testament apocrypha and pseudepigrapha, asking similar questions.

Here we can see that the concordance provides us a way of examining important terms and concepts as they are used in the biblical writings. By looking up the passages and engaging in aggressive and creative interrogation of the material, we expand our understanding and provide ourselves with perspectives from which to approach the passage.

Using the concordance in this way recognizes the fact that the texts in which a term occurs provide the context in which it should be understood. In fact, wordbooks, lexicons, and other studies focusing on single terms or phrases are prepared using the concordance as the basic tool. To save time, we may bypass the concordance work by consulting such works first, yet the task of consulting the texts themselves directly should not be handed over too quickly to someone else. For one thing, this will make it more difficult for us to make primary discoveries which the wordbooks may have missed or to critique the conclusions drawn in the wordbooks. Also, if we skip this all important primary level of investigation, the resulting exegesis will tend to be derivative rather than original. Actually, it is better for us to do the primary investigative work first, formulate our own hypotheses and interpretive explanations based on these observations, and then use the wordbooks and similar tools as checks on our own insights and findings.

We are not able, at this point, to mention all the ways in which a concordance can be used in exegesis. We can only repeat that it is perhaps the single most valuable resource for the exegete who wishes to do original work on a passage.

In using the above mentioned tools, a special problem arises when the investigation moves beyond the English language to the original Hebrew or Greek. As noted earlier, the student without knowledge of the original language can still make use of most of these tools, although knowledge of the languages will obviously be an advantage.

The following suggestions may be offered at this point for the student without a knowledge of the biblical languages. First, as mentioned earlier, some concordances based on English translations of the Bible, although listing the English words, provide the Hebrew or Greek word which the English word translates, and in most cases transliterate the original word into English. Thus, the English-speaking student can at least determine the transliterated form of the original word. Second, since a single Hebrew or Greek word is usually rendered by several English words, the analytical concordances provide appendixes containing comprehensive indexes of these terms and their various English renderings. The terms in the concordances are coded for making reference to the appendixes. Third, recent editions of concordances have begun to be keyed so that they are correlated with lexicons and wordbooks. Thus the student can move from the word in the English text to the concordances to the lexicons and wordbooks. This makes it possible to find the word being studied in a Hebrew or Greek lexicon, even without knowing the Hebrew or Greek alphabet. Fourth, a student may determine the original Hebrew or Greek word by consulting an interlinear, an edition of the Bible which provides the original text of the Bible on one line and an English translation on an adjacent line.

Moving from the English to the original Hebrew or Greek is not an easy process, nor is it obvious in every case, but the diligent student who has access to basic tools for biblical exegesis can make this transition. By careful use of such resources, and by consulting with those who know the original languages, it is possible to gain access to this body of information which will help to illuminate the language of the text.

In performing word studies and using biblical wordbooks, lexicons, and dictionaries, the student should be aware that potentially fallacious conclusions can be drawn from such studies. Certain linguistic principles should be kept in mind to keep from engaging in faulty word studies and reaching wrongly based conclusions.

(1) Words in Hebrew, Aramaic, and Greek, just as words in any language, frequently possess a wide variety of meanings. Modern-language dictionaries tend to offer a number of meanings for words rather than giving a single meaning from which all others are assumed to derive. Unfortunately, many biblical wordbooks give the impression that biblical terms had a single basic meaning that was "carried" in the root form of the word. This assumption is known as the "root fallacy." Even though utilized in many studies, this hypothesis about root meanings should be avoided.

(2) Biblical writers and characters were no more aware of the history of the words and expressions they used than are modern writers and speakers. Very few of us are aware of the history of the words we use nor do we try to determine what the "original meaning" of a word was before using it. Unless we are historical philologists, such matters are seldom more than a curiosity. What matters is whether the words we are using communicate what we want to say. Students should not assume that "original meanings" exist for words, that ancient users were aware of such, and that some "original meaning" must be discerned whenever a word appears.

(3) Generally individual words or phrases are not in themselves the bearers of special theological meaning. The student should avoid assuming that when a term, even a technical one, occurs that the original reader automatically was conscious of a host of theological concepts, much less a theological system. The term "covenant," for example, was used in diverse contexts in ancient Israel and its appearance in a text should not automatically be taken to be a reference to a special divine-human relationship. Similarly, the New Testament word for love, *agape*, should not automatically be taken to mean some special form of self-giving concern (see Luke 11:43).

(4) An idea or theological concept can be expressed in one way with

one set of terms in one text and the same or similar idea or concept expressed in another way with another set of terms in a different text. It should not be assumed that ideas or concepts can only be expressed with one set of terms.

(5) The best guide to the meaning of a word is the context in which it is used. This means, first of all, the immediate context of the passage in which it occurs. If a word has several meanings, one should explore the range of meanings and see how they fit or do not fit in the context. A broader context is the whole of the document in which the terms appear. One should explore how a term is used and what it denotes elsewhere in the document. A further context is the biblical and non-biblical documents contemporary with the document being studied. Since the meaning and use of words change through history, one should avoid taking the meaning of a word in one historical or even documentary context and assuming a similar meaning in another time or place. We all recognize that some of the terms used in the KJV now mean something totally different.

As we mentioned earlier, the language of the text consists not only of words, but words arranged in meaningful combinations. Consequently, grammatical criticism also includes questions of language, syntax, and grammar. Here the exegete deals with the words of the text as they are combined with each other to form phrases, sentences, and paragraphs as well as the special problems this creates.

A sound knowledge of English grammar serves as a valuable prerequisite for this level of interpretation, but because English instruction in schools at both the secondary and college level have de-emphasized explicit aspects of English grammar over the past several years, many beginning exegetes encounter a special difficulty here. While such students may use good grammar, their knowledge of grammatical rules may not be sufficiently explicit to allow them to analyze and discuss the grammar of the English Bible. Because of this, it may be necessary for the beginning exegete to consult a standard English composition or grammar book before other exegetical tools will be of much use. For example, one will need to possess elementary knowledge of parts of speech and basic grammatical terms to analyze the syntax of a passage.

Questions of syntax and grammar often arise when we try to discern the meaning of a sense unit. Such questions can surface as we merely compare two or more English translations and notice the various ways in which the passage is actually rendered into English. Translators' footnotes may also provide indications of such questions. Two examples may be noted. In 2 Corinthians 5:19, the RSV reads "in Christ God was reconciling the world to himself." An alternative translation is provided in the note: "God was in Christ reconciling (the world to himself)." Consulting other translations, such as the NEB, points up the exegetical difficulty even further. The exegetical significance is far-reaching: the former lays greater stress on the act of reconciliation as initiated by God while the latter lays greater stress on Christ as the locus and agent of reconciliation. The exegete must decide whether the passage is fundamentally a soteriological statement about salvation as an act of grace initiated by God, or a fundamentally christological statement about the incarnation. In this case, the meaning of the words themselves pose no exegetical difficulty. It is rather their combination with each other, that is, their syntax, that provides the exegetical difficulty.

A similar exegetical problem is presented in the opening verse of Genesis, which the RSV renders "In the beginning God created the heavens and the earth." The alternative translation, "When God began to create," is possible because of a different assessment of the grammatical evidence. As before, the other translations point to the same exegetical problem.

To resolve such questions, we must inevitably deal with the grammar and syntax of the passage. This becomes evident when one consults critical commentaries on the passage where the various options are outlined and discussed. Eventually, it may be necessary to consult standard grammars of the Hebrew and Greek languages.

Quite often, it may be useful to diagram the passage. Older methods of diagramming sentences, used in English composition courses, may prove useful in this regard, but the system of diagramming need not be conventional or even highly structured. What is often needed, more than anything else, is for the student to rewrite the passage, diagramming it in a series of sense-units, in order to see how the various parts relate to each other. In this way, it often becomes clear that certain phrases can be located in one or more places, each altering the interpretation of the sentence. This is a very worthwhile practice if the text is poetic, for we may discover parallel structures not otherwise obvious, especially if the text is printed as straight prose in the English edition of the Bible one is using.

Analyzing the syntax of the passage and assessing grammatical rules as they apply to the passage should only be done insofar as the text requires it. Some texts require little or no grammatical analysis of this sort, while others, such as some passages in Paul's writings, will be difficult to understand any other way.

It should be stressed that this facet of exegesis deals with the author's world of thought as it is expressed through written words. The language of the text provides the skeletal structure of the author's thought and grammatical criticism assists the exegete in entering and making sense of particular portions of the author's thought-world in its own right and in relating these to other aspects of the same author's thought as well as to the Bible as a whole.

BIBLIOGRAPHY

Old Testament Lexicons and Aids

Brown, F., S. R. Driver, and C. A. Briggs, *A Hebrew and English Lexicon of the Old Testament* (corrected ed.; London/New York: Oxford University Press, 1952; reissued as *The New Brown, Driver, and Briggs . . . Numerically Coded to Strong's Exhaustive Concordance*, Grand Rapids: Baker Book House, 1981).

Davidson, B., *The Analytical Hebrew and Chaldee Lexicon* (London: Samuel Bagster & Sons, 1848, often reprinted by various publishers).

Einspahr, B., *Index to Brown, Driver and Briggs Hebrew Lexicon* (Chicago: Moody Press, 1976).

Gesenius' Hebrew and Chaldee Lexicon to the Old Testament Scriptures: Numerically Coded to Strong's Exhaustive Concordance (Grand Rapids: Baker Book House, 1979).

*Holladay, W. L., *A Concise Hebrew and Aramaic Lexicon of the Old Testament, Based upon the Lexical Work of L. Koehler and W. Baumgartner* (Leiden/Grand Rapids: E. J. Brill/Eerdmans Publishing Company, 1971).

Jastrow, M., *A Dictionary of the Targumin, the Talmud Babli and Yerushalmi, and the Midrashic Literature* (London/New York: Luzac/Putman, 1886–1900; often reprinted by various publishers).

Koehler, L. and W. Baumgartner, *Lexicon in Veteris Testamenti libros* (2d ed.; Leiden: E. J. Brill, 1958).

Robinson, M. A., *Indexes to All Editions of Brown-Driver-Briggs Hebrew Lexicon and Thayer's Greek Lexicon* (Grand Rapids: Baker Book House, 1981).

New Testament Lexicons and Aids

Abbott-Smith, G., *A Manual Greek Lexicon of the New Testament* (3d ed.; Edinburgh: T. & T. Clark, 1937).

Alsop, J. R., *An Index to the Bauer-Arndt-Gingrich Greek Lexicon* (2d ed.: Grand Rapids: Zondervan Publishing House, 1981).

*Bauer, W., F. W. Gingrich, and F. W. Danker, *A Greek-English Lexicon of the New Testament and Other Early Christian Literature* (Chicago/London: University of Chicago Press, 1979).

Bullinger, E. W., *A Critical Lexicon and Concordance to the English and Greek New Testament* (London: Longmans & Co., 1877; last edition reissued, London/Grand Rapids: Samuel Bagster and Sons Ltd./Zondervan Publishing House, 1975).

Friberg, B. and T. Friberg, *Analytical Greek New Testament* (Grand Rapids: Baker Book House, 1981).

Kubo, S., *A Reader's Greek Lexicon of the New Testament* (Berrien Springs/ Edinburgh: Andrews University Press/T. & T. Clark, 1971/1979).

Liddell, H. G. and R. Scott, *A Greek-English Lexicon: A New Edition Revised and Augmented Throughout with Supplement* (9th ed.; London: Oxford University Press, 1925–1940; Supplement, 1968).

Moulton, H. K., *The Analytical Greek Lexicon Revised* (London/Grand Rapids: Samuel Bagster and Sons Ltd./Zondervan Publishing House, 1977/1978).

Moulton, J. H. and G. Milligan, *The Vocabulary of the Greek Testament, Illustrated from the Papyri and Other Non-Literary Sources* (2d ed.; London/ Grand Rapids: Hodder and Stoughton/Eerdmans Publishing Company, 1957/ 1963).

Rienecker, F., *A Linguistic Key to the Greek Testament* (2 vols.; Grand Rapids: Zondervan Publishing House, 1976–1980).

Thayer, J. H., *A Greek-English Lexicon of the New Testament: A Dictionary Numerically Coded to Strong's Exhaustive Concordance* (Grand Rapids: Baker Book House, 1977).

Zerwick, M. and M. Grosvenor, *A Grammatical Analysis of the Greek New Testament* (2 vols.; Rome: Biblical Institute Press, 1974–1979).

Hebrew and Aramaic Grammars

Gesenius, W. and E. Kautzsch, *Gesenius' Hebrew Grammar* (2d ed.; London/ New York: Oxford University Press, 1910; 15th printing [1980] has a revised index of passages).

*Greenberg, M., *Introduction to Hebrew* (Englewood Cliffs: Prentice-Hall, 1965).

Johns, A. F., *A Short Grammar of Biblical Aramaic* (Berrien Springs: Andrews University Press, 1972).

*Lambdin, T. O., *Introduction to Biblical Hebrew* (New York/London: Charles Scribner's Sons/Darton, Longman and Todd, 1971/1973).

*Rosenthal, F. A., *A Grammar of Biblical Aramaic* (Wiesbaden: Harrassowitz, 1961).

*Sawyer, J. F. A., *A Modern Introduction to Biblical Hebrew* (Stocksfield: Oriel Press, 1976).

Weingreen, J., *Practical Grammar for Classical Hebrew* (2d ed.; New York/ London: Oxford University Press, 1959).

Williams, R. J., *Hebrew Syntax: An Outline* (2d ed.; Toronto/Buffalo/London: University of Toronto Press, 1976).

Greek Grammars

Blass, F., A. Debrunner, and R. W. Funk, *A Greek Grammar of the New Testament and Other Early Christian Literature* (Chicago/London: University of Chicago Press, 1961).

Funk, R. W., *A Beginning-Intermediate Grammar of Hellenistic Greek* (3 vols.; 2d ed.; Missoula: Scholars Press, 1977).

*Machen, J. G., *New Testament Greek for Beginners* (New York: Macmillan Co., 1944).

Moule, C. F. D., *An Idiom-Book of New Testament Greek* (2d ed.; London/New York: Cambridge University Press, 1959).

Moulton, J. H., F. W. Howard, and N. Turner, *A Grammar of New Testament Greek* (4 vols.; Edinburgh: T. & T. Clark, 1929–1976).

Owings, J., *A Cumulative Index to New Testament Greek Grammars* (Grand Rapids: Baker Book House, 1983).

Robertson, A. T., *A Grammar of the Greek New Testament in the Light of Historical Research* (4th ed.; Nashville/London: Broadman Press/Hodder and Stoughton, 1923).

*Smyth, H. W., *Greek Grammar* (rev. ed.; Cambridge: Harvard University Press, 1963).

Thackeray, H. St. J., *A Grammar of the Old Testament in Greek According to the Septuagint* (vol. 1; London: Cambridge University Press, 1909).

Concordances

Aland, K., *Vollständige Konkordanz zum griechischen Neuen Testament: Unter Zugrundelegung aller kritischen Textausgaben und des Textus Receptus* (2 vols.; Berlin/New York, Walter de Gruyter, 1975–   ).

Bachmann, H. and H. Slaby (eds.), *Computer-Konkordanz zum Novum Testamentum Graece von Nestle-Aland, 26. Auflage, und zum Greek New Testament* (3d ed.; Berlin/New York: Walter de Gruyter, 1980).

*Bailey, L. R., "What a Concordance Can Do for You " in *Biblical Archaeology Review* 10/6 (1984) 60–67.

Concordance to the Apocrypha/Deuterocanonical Books of the Revised Standard Version (Grand Rapids: Eerdmans Publishing Company, 1982).

Cruden, A., *Complete Concordance to the Old and New Testaments* (Guildford/Grand Rapids: Lutterworth Press/Baker Book House, 1930/1953).

Darton, M., *Modern Concordance to the New Testament* (London/Garden City: Darton, Longman and Todd/Doubleday, 1976).

Davidson, B., *A Concordance of the Hebrew and Chaldee Scriptures* (London: Samuel Bagster & Sons, 1876).

Ellison, J. W., *Nelson's Complete Concordance of the Revised Standard Version Bible* (2d ed.; New York/London: Thomas Nelson, 1972).

Even-Shoshan, A., *A New Concordance of the Old Testament: Using the Hebrew and Aramaic Text* (Jerusalem/Grand Rapids: "Kiryat Sepher" Publishing House/Baker Book House, 1982/1984).

Goodrick, E. W. and J. R. Kohlenberger, *The NIV Complete Concordance* (Grand Rapids: Zondervan Publishing House, 1981).

Hartdegen, S. J., *Nelson's Complete Concordance of the New American Bible* (Collegeville/Nashville: Liturgical Press/Thomas Nelson, Inc., 1977).

Hatch, E. and H. A. Redpath, *A Concordance to the Septuagint and the Other Greek Versions of the Old Testament Including the Apocryphal Books* (3 vols.; London: Oxford University Press, 1897–1906; reprinted in 2 vols., Graz: Akademischer Druck, 1954). (See also *An Expanded Index of the Hatch-Redpath Concordance to the Septuagint* [Jerusalem: Dugith Publishers, 1974].)

Lisowsky, G., *Konkordanz zum hebräischen Alten Testament* (2d ed.; Stuttgart: Württembergische Bibelanstalt, 1958).

Mandelkern, S., *Veteris Testamenti concordantiae hebraicae atque chaldaicae* (9th ed.; Jerusalem/Tel Aviv: Schocken, 1971).

Morgenthaler, R., *Statistik des neutestamentlicher Wortschatzes* (2d ed.; Zurich: Gotthelf Verlag, 1973).

Morrish, G., *Concordance of the Septuagint* (reprinted; Grand Rapids: Baker Book House, 1976).

*Morrison, C., *An Analytical Concordance to the Revised Standard Version of the New Testament* (Philadelphia/London: Westminster Press/SCM Press, 1979).

Moulton, W. F. and A. S. Geden, *A Concordance to the Greek Testament According to the Texts of Westcott and Hort, Tischendorf and the English Revisers* (5th ed., rev. by H. K. Moulton, with a supplement; Edinburgh: T. & T. Clark, 1978).

Schmoller, A., *Handkonkordanz zum griechischen Neuen Testament* (9th ed.; Stuttgart: Württembergische Bibelanstalt, 1951).

Strong, J., *The Exhaustive Concordance of the Bible* (New York/Cincinnati: Hunt Eaton/Cranston Curts, 1894; frequently reprinted by various publishers).

Wigram, G. V., *The Englishman's Greek Concordance Numerically Coded to Strong's Exhaustive Concordance* (Grand Rapids: Baker Book House, 1979).

Wigram, G. V., *The Englishman's Hebrew and Chaldee Concordance of the Old Testament Numerically Coded to Strong's Exhaustive Concordance* (Grand Rapids: Baker Book House, 1980).

Wigram, G. V. and R. D. Winter, *The Word Study Concordance* (Wheaton/Pasadena: Tyndale House Publishers/William Carey Library, 1978; keyed to Strong, Moulton-Geden, Arndt-Gingrich, and Kittel-Friedrich).

*Young, R., *Analytical Concordance to the Bible* (8th ed.; London/New York: Lutterworth Press/Funk and Wagnalls, 1939; reissued by other publishers).

Wordbooks

von Allmen, J. J. (ed.), *The Vocabulary of the Bible: A Companion to the Bible* (London/New York: Lutterworth Press/Oxford University Press, 1958).

Bauer, J. B. (ed.), *Sacramentum verbi: An Encyclopedia of Biblical Theology* (3 vols,; London/New York: Sheed and Ward/Herder and Herder, 1970).

*Botterweck, J. and H. Ringgren (eds.), *Theological Dictionary of the Old Testament* (Grand Rapids/London: Ecrdmans Publishing Company/SCM Press, 1977–   ).

Brown, C. (ed.), *The New International Dictionary of New Testament Theology* (3 vols.; Grand Rapids/Exeter: Zondervan Publishing House/Paternoster Press, 1975–1978).

*Kittel, G. and G. Friedrich (eds.), *Theological Dictionary of the New Testament* (10 vols.; Grand Rapids/London: Eerdmans Publishing Company/SCM Press, 1964–1976; 1-volume abridged ed., 1985).

Léon-Dufour, X., *Dictionary of Biblical Theology* (rev. ed.; London/New York: Geoffrey Chapman/Seabury Press, 1973).

*Richardson, A. (ed.), *A Theological Word Book of the Bible* (London/New York: SCM Press/Macmillan Company, 1950/1951).

Robertson, A. T., *Word Pictures in the New Testament* (6 vols.; New York/London: Harper & Brothers, 1930–1933).

Turner, N., *Grammatical Insights into the New Testament* (Edinburgh: T. & T. Clark, 1965).

Turner, N., *Christian Words* (Edinburgh/Nashville: T. & T. Clark/Thomas Nelson Publishers, 1981/1982).

Vincent, M. R., *Word Studies in the New Testament* (4 vols.; New York/London: Charles Scribner's Sons, 1887–1900; reprinted, Grand Rapids: Eerdmans Publishing Company, 1946).

Vine, W. F., *Expository Dictionary of New Testament Words* (4 vols.; London: Oliphants, 1939–1941; reissued in 1 vol., London/Grand Rapids: Marshall, Morgan & Scott/Zondervan Publishing House, 1952/1981).

Interlinears

Berry, G. R. and J. Strong, *Interlinear Greek-English New Testament Numerically Coded to Strong's Exhaustive Concordance* (Grand Rapids: Baker Book House, 1981).

*Green, J. (ed. and tr.), *The Interlinear Bible: Hebrew/English* (Grand Rapids: Baker Book House, 1979).

Kohlenberger, J. R., *The NIV Interlinear Hebrew-English Old Testament* (4 vols.; Grand Rapids: Zondervan Publishing House, 1979–).

*Marshall, A., *The R.S.V. Interlinear Greek-English New Testament* (London/Grand Rapids: Samuel Bagster and Sons Ltd./Zondervan Publishing House, 1968/1970).

Semantics and Linguistics

Barr, J., *Comparative Philology and the Text of the Old Testament* (London/New York: Oxford University Press, 1968).

*Barr, J., *The Semantics of Biblical Language* (London/New York: Oxford University Press, 1961).

Caird, G. B., *The Language and Imagery of the Bible* (London/Philadelphia: Gerald Duckworth & Co., Ltd./Westminster Press, 1980).

Gibson, A., *Biblical Semantic Logic: A Preliminary Analysis* (Oxford/New York: Basil Blackwell/St. Martin's Press, 1981).

Louw, J. P., *Semantics of New Testament Greek* (Chico/Philadelphia: Scholars Press/Fortress Press, 1982).

Nida, E. A. and C. R. Taber, *The Theory and Practice of Translation* (2d ed.; Leiden: E. J. Brill, 1982).

Sawyers, J. F. A., *Semantics in Biblical Research* (London: SCM Press, 1972).

Taber, C. R., "Semantics" in *Interpreter's Dictionary of the Bible, Supplementary Volume*, 800–807.

CHAPTER 5

LITERARY CRITICISM:

The Composition and Rhetorical Style of the Text

In its broadest sense, literary criticism encompasses all questions which arise pertaining to the text itself, including its authorship, historical setting, and various aspects of the language and content of the text. (Many of these issues we have treated in the two previous chapters because they constitute separate tasks in their own right.)

Historically, "literary criticism" in traditional biblical studies has had a rather narrow focus referring primarily to source or documentary analysis. This attitude had its origins in the eighteenth century. When biblical interpreters became increasingly aware of difficulties in reading particular portions of the scriptures, they intuited that certain books (such as 2 Corinthians) and certain blocks of material (such as the Pentateuch) were composites of various documents. They were secondary collections of earlier smaller works. The attempts to isolate these various documents gave birth to source criticism. The tasks of separating out these sources or layers, of describing their content and characteristic features, and of relating them to one another eventually came to be designated "literary criticism."

In general literary studies, "literary criticism" denotes a broad range of topics: the compositional structure and character of a text, techniques of style, the employment of images and symbols by an author, aesthetic and dramatic effects in a work, and so on. All of these factors are involved in reading and understanding biblical texts. The Bible may be more than literature but it is certainly literature. And in this regard, the Bible should be read like any other body of literature. As with literature in general, one must read the Bible with some literary competence and discretion. We all realize that different reading conventions are operative depending on whether one is reading prose and narrative or poetry and verse. Different kinds of literature are capable of having different kinds of meaning and supply different kinds of "information" to the reader. This means that different questions must be asked in interrogating different types of literature.

Closely related to literary criticism is rhetorical criticism. Rhetoric is one of the oldest academic disciplines. It is concerned with how a speaker advocates a position and seeks to convince an audience or reader of the validity of that position. Although originally concerned with oratory and spoken presentations, rhetoric was applicable to written texts since most ancient texts, although written, were composed to be read aloud.

Most biblical literature is what might be called "purposeful" literature. It seeks to persuade the reader about certain truths, positions, and courses of action and is thus subject to rhetorical analysis. Much biblical literature was produced for very particular situations. Paul, for example, wrote his letters to address special conditions in the life of early Christian communities. The ancient prophets as well delivered their speeches in particular historical and social contexts. These particular occasions and contexts are what can be called rhetorical situations. A rhetorical situation involves an audience, a speaker or writer, a topic or issue of mutual concern, and an occasion for communication. In a rhetorical situation, the communicator (speaker/writer) seeks to convince or persuade the audience to accept some particular interpretation or course of action.

The study of rhetoric was highly developed and discussed among the ancient Greeks. Rhetorical skills were certainly developed and cherished in Old Testament times even though we do not know how these were taught. According to Aristotle, rhetoric was the faculty for discovering the best means of persuasion. As such, rhetoric was taught in schools as involving five steps: (1) invention—the planning of a discourse and the arguments and evidence to be employed in it; (2) arrangement—the ordering of the component parts to produce an effective whole; (3) style—the choice of the means and methods for expressing the discourse; (4) memory— preparation for delivery; and (5) delivery—matters related to voice and gestures in the presentation. In written discourse, only the first three steps were involved.

Ancient rhetoric paid particular attention to the nature of proof in developing persuasive discourse. Aristotle discussed different modes of proof depending upon whether they focused on the speaker, the audience, or the discourse. These different forms centered on ethos, pathos, and logos. Ethos denotes "character" and has to do with the speaker's or writer's credibility and trustworthiness. Biblical authors' use of ethical appeal can be seen, for example, in Paul's frequent autobiographical references and in the prophets' reports of their experiences. Evidence, such as the quotation of Scripture or tradition or the ever-present list in 1 and 2 Chronicles, lends credibility to the author. Pathos has to do with the feelings and reactions of the audience. Much of the imagery of the Bible seeks to appeal to the audience's emotions and feelings and thus to gain a hearing and a response. Exaggeration and hyperbole abound. Logos has to do with logical developments within the discourse. Various forms of logic, both inductive and deductive, may be found in any purposeful, persuasive text.

In exegeting a biblical text, we must be alert to the literary and rhetorical dimensions of a text. Emphasis on compositional techniques and rhetorical features aid in understanding how a writing has been developed, how its structure and style contribute to its presentation, and what objectives the writer may have had in mind.

Literary criticism of biblical texts recognizes that a single text, passage, or pericope generally forms a part of a larger whole—the document of which it is a part. As a component in a larger whole, the part both contributes to the meaning of the whole and derives meaning from the sense of the whole. A passage in Romans or a narrative in Genesis, for example, can best be properly exegeted when they are viewed as components within their larger contexts. In these two cases, obviously the larger contexts are the books of Genesis and Romans. A text, however, usually has a number of literary contexts. There is, of course, the immediate context of the passage or its location between what precedes and what follows. The passage and its immediate context may be components within a larger sub-unit of a book and a book may be composed of several such sub-units. At the same time, however, even a book may be part of a larger unit or whole, that is, it may be part of a multi-book document, such as Luke–Acts or 1 and 2 Chronicles.

In attempting to understand a particular text, the exegete should seek to see the text within the structure of the major context as well as within the structure of the sub-units. Reading through an entire document, constructing an outline, and consulting the outlines given in commentaries and other works can aid in determining the general structure and style of the larger work and the compositional techniques employed in its production.

Ancient authors and collectors, like their modern counterparts, could use various compositional techniques to give structural outline to their works and to tie together various internal sub-units and blocks of material. The structure of individual works might be based on such considerations as thematic interests, chronological schemes (most historical books), plot or plot motifs (particularly all narrative), particular apologetic or defense argumentation (many of the letters of Paul), alphabetic lines in which the successive letters of the alphabet are used to give an external arrangement to material (several of the psalms, Lamentations), speeches and summations (Deuteronomy—2 Kings, Matthew), geographical references (much of Exodus—Numbers), association of subject matter (Old Testament law codes), patterns dictated by use in rituals and worship (many of the psalms), and so on. Frequently the structure of a text may reflect the operation of several of these techniques. Often the shape of a text also reflects standard forms and genres characteristic of the author's time and thus is not the special creation of the writer. (This will be discussed further in the chapter on form criticism.)

The structuring of material was not only characteristic of books and large complexes but also of major blocks and sub-units within works. Individual component parts within a document might have their own particular structure. The text being exegeted thus needs to be considered in light of both major and minor structural complexes.

Because ancient authors and collectors often incorporated preexisting materials and sources into their works, the structure and outline of internal blocks of material may have derived from the structure of the earlier sources. Thus one can encounter multilayered structures within the same document. In a heavily edited work like the Pentateuch, the exegete encounters both the structure of the earlier sources and the structure of the final form of the text. Ideally, a particular text can best be exegeted when its place and function can be seen within each of the layers or sources of the text. Thus a passage found in the Pentateuch can be viewed not only in terms of its present context in the final form of the text but also in terms of its context in the earlier sources (the so-called J, E, D, and P documents). In like fashion, various layers of tradition can be seen in the Synoptic Gospels. The earliest Gospel writer, probably Mark, inherited cycles of tradition which were given new meaning when combined with other materials into a gospel form. In like manner, when Mark's material was utilized by Matthew and Luke, the traditions were again given another context and became incorporated into these works with different structures and compositional techniques.

Various factors in a document may indicate the use and incorporation of sources. Among these are (1) changes in literary style, (2) shifts in vocabulary, (3) breaks in continuity of thought or presentation, (4) the presence of secondary linking and connecting statements, (5) changes in theological and other viewpoints, (6) duplications or repetition of material, (7) clearly defined and isolatable sub-units, and (8) chronological, factual, or other inconsistencies. Utilizing these indications, the exegete can often isolate earlier sources. As we have noted, much of nineteenth-century literary criticism focused on this isolation of sources and their dating and original historical contexts.

Biblical scholarship has sought to establish the overall literary structure of most of the biblical writings and the sources which may lie behind and be incorporated in them. As one would expect, disagreement exists over how individual works should be divided and subdivided, but discussion of these disagreements in critical introductions and other handbooks is often quite useful in providing the student with the sorts of options available. In addition, the introductory sections to commentaries on individual books often provide the student with information pertaining to literary markers within the text which indicate structural divisions and structuring techniques. These various markers in the text note such things as the beginning and ending of sections or transitions within sections. Some of these are temporal, others geographical or spatial; some are technical or formulaic while others may be subtle.

As important as it is to consult reference works, however, it is equally, perhaps more, important for the exegete who has established the larger literary unit within which the text occurs, whether it is a single book or a major division within a book, to read this larger literary unit, not once but several times. This will assist the reader in determining even more precisely how the passage being exegeted fits into the larger whole and how it functions within this whole.

Questions of literary function which the exegete should ask are: How does the particular passage function with respect to its immediate and larger context? Is it transitional, that is, does it serve as a literary bridge from one section to another? Is it climactic, that is, does it serve as the culmination of several paragraphs or sections immediately preceding it? Is it illustrative, that is, does it function to illustrate an earlier assertion? Is it extrinsic to the larger literary unit, that is, does it not fit at all into the literary context?

By asking such questions as these the interpreter is seeking to relate the passage to its larger literary context by establishing connections within the text. Doing so is an important aspect of exegesis because clues to interpreting the passage often lie outside the passage itself and are found in its larger literary setting. For example, if one is exegeting

Luke's account of Jesus' initial sermon in Nazareth (see Luke 4:16–30), by viewing it in relation to the document as a whole, one discovers that the passage is not presented simply as another event in the ministry of Jesus, but rather as an inaugural event. Its placement at this point in Luke's account makes it crucial in the overall development of the story. Major literary and theological themes developed later in Luke-Acts are introduced at this point, yet it is only by reading the document as a whole that one can recognize how many important Lukan themes converge here as well as how they are developed elsewhere in the narrative. To cite another example, the middle section of Paul's epistle to the Romans, chapters 9—11, must be viewed in relation to the whole letter. And, one can safely say, what the interpreter finally decides about how these three chapters relate to the rest of the letter ultimately determines how the entire letter is interpreted. If, for example, the exegete concludes that these three chapters are a digression and thus only incidental to the over-all contents of the letter, the letter will be read one way. If, by contrast, these three chapters are seen as the culmination of everything that has gone before in chapters 1—8, the letter will be read another way. Thus, establishing the literary function of a given text becomes a crucial step in exegeting the passage.

Questions of the literary placement and function of a passage can sometimes be formulated helpfully in another way. The interpreter can ask: What effect would it have on the document as a whole if the passage were omitted entirely? Would something be irretrievably lost? Or, would nothing substantially important be lost? What effect would it have on the document if the passage were relocated and placed somewhere else in the document? How would this affect the overall structure and content of the document?

By asking questions about the literary placement and function of the passage, the interpreter often is able to detect certain things about the passage otherwise missed. For example, by looking at the immediate literary context, one may discover that the passage is one of a series of prophetic oracles, each of which has a particular function within a larger sequence, or one of a series of miracle stories, each of which serves to unfold some aspect of a messianic portrait. By placing the passage in its larger literary context, the interpreter will not only be better able to understand the passage in its own right, its particular nuances and distinctive content, but also the larger document as a whole. As we noted earlier, a passage both shares in the meaning of the larger literary unit and contributes to it.

By examining a passage in its relation to its larger literary context, the exegete leaves open the possibility that the author or collector sought carefully to construct the document as a whole in order to achieve maximum effect. Quite often, ancient authors employed rhetorical techniques and devices within the text itself to assist in the comprehension of the message of the text and to persuade the hearer or reader of the truth of its presentation. Because the biblical writings were written originally to be read aloud, this rhetorical dimension of the text was an important ingredient in composition. By contrast, because silent reading is more often the norm in modern times than oral reading, these rhetorical dimensions are often overlooked by the modern reader. Yet, they are extremely valuable to the exegete in understanding the biblical writings.

The Gospel of Matthew has always been noted for its balance and symmetry. The author's fondness for organizing information in groups of sevens and threes is well known. Organizing the story of Jesus in this manner certainly made it easier to remember the information, and catechetical considerations may have been one of the primary factors in determining how the book was organized. Consequently, the interpreter, for example, should allow for the possibility that the group of seven parables found in chapter 13 represents the author's arrangement rather than reflects an actual historical situation. In this instance, giving attention to the rhetorical or compositional aspect of the text will bear directly on historical questions.

Similarly, because ancient authors were aware of the difficulty hearers and readers had in following an extended argument or narrative, they would often supply periodic summaries throughout the narrative to assist the reader in "catching up" with the story or argument. Numerous instances of this occur in the book of Acts, for example.

Various techniques were used for structuring not only individual units but also entire documents. A frequently used structural device was known as "chiasmus," a principle of arranging materials in a symmetrical pattern where certain components would correspond to other components. In a four-part arrangement, the chiastic structure might follow an a-b-b-a pattern, where the first and fourth items corresponded to each other while the second and third items did so as well. Another such device was what is called "inclusio." This refers to the practice of restating or paraphrasing the opening and leading idea or phrase at the conclusion in order to reemphasize the point being made or the position being advocated. These devices were widely used in antiquity and are found frequently in the biblical writings.

Knowing that ancient writers often employed rhetorical techniques and devices may assist the interpreter in understanding the structure of a document. For one thing, the overall structure may be unfamiliar and incomprehensible to the modern reader because it does not easily fit into *modern* notions of sequence and organization; yet, it may fit perfectly into *ancient* notions of arrangement. A document may be perfectly symmetrical and logically sequential, provided one understands the rhetorical principle or principles upon which it was based.

Another aspect of literary criticism should also be mentioned in conclusion—literary mood. Language is often used as much to create effect as it is to convey information in a straightforward manner. Beginning exegetes often err in over-analyzing the words and phrases within a passage without detecting the more subtle ways in which the language is functioning. The phrase "You are rich!" (1 Cor. 4:8) read as a straight declarative sentence means one thing, but read as irony means quite the opposite. Similarly, biblical statements often convey a quality other than straightforward declaration. The Fourth Gospel, for example, is highly ironical both in its overall structure and in individual stories within the Gospel, and the exegete's task cannot ignore this dimension of literary mood. The mood of one text may be liturgical, in which case the language may be more poetic, less direct, and intended to elicit certain emotions rather than convey theological information. Accordingly, how one understands individual words or phrases in a highly evocative passage exuding the atmosphere of worship may differ radically from how one understands the same words or phrases within a text whose mood is fiercely polemical or apologetic. To read a piece of comedy as straightforward narrative is itself comic, and the exegete does well to be attentive to these more unspoken dimensions of the text.

The literary criticism of a biblical text, thus, focuses on the "world of the text," its composition, its structure, its style, and its mood. Numerous studies are available to assist the exegete in this type of investigation. Nothing, however, is more crucial than the ability to read a text thoroughly, closely, sympathetically, with both an eye and an ear to the internal dimensions of the text which may serve as most useful clues to understanding.

BIBLIOGRAPHY

General

*Alter, R., *The Art of Biblical Narrative* (New York/London: Basic Books, Inc./ Allen & Unwin, 1981).

*Alter, R., *The Art of Biblical Poetry* (New York/London: Basic Books, Inc./ Allen & Unwin, 1985).

Auerbach, E., "Odysseus' Scar," in his *Mimesis: The Representation of Reality in Western Literature* (Princeton: Princeton University Press, 1953) 1–23.

Barr, J., "Reading the Bible as Literature" in *Bulletin of the John Rylands University Library* 56 (1973) 10–33.

*Beardslee, W., *Literary Criticism of the New Testament* (Philadelphia: Fortress Press, 1970).

Crossan, J. D. (ed.), *Paul Ricoeur on Biblical Hermeneutics* (*Semeia* 4; Missoula: Scholars Press, 1975).

Fishbane, M., *Text and Texture: Close Readings of Selected Biblical Texts* (New York: Schocken Books, 1979).

Frye, N., *The Great Code: The Bible and Literature* (New York/London: Harcourt Brace Jovanovich, 1982).

Funk, R. W., *Language, Hermeneutic, and Word of God* (New York: Harper & Row, 1966).

Funk, R. W., (ed.), *Literary Critical Studies of Biblical Texts* (*Semeia* 8; Missoula: Scholars Press, 1977).

Gottcent, J. H., *The Bible as Literature: A Selective Bibliography* (Boston: G. K. Hall & Co., 1979).

Habel, N., *Literary Criticism of the Old Testament* (Philadelphia: Fortress Press, 1971).

*Juel, D., with J.S. Ackerman and T. S. Warshaw, *An Introduction to New Testament Literature* (Nashville: Abingdon Press, 1978).

Long, B. O. (ed.), *Images of Man and God: Old Testament Short Stories in Literary Focus* (Sheffield: JSOT Press, 1981).

*Louis, K. R., J. S. Ackerman, and T. S. Warshaw, *Literary Interpretations of Biblical Narratives* (2 vols.; Nashville: Abingdon Press, 1974, 1982).

McKnight, E. V., *Meaning in Texts: The Historical Shaping of a Narrative Hermeneutics* (Philadelphia: Fortress Press, 1978).

McKnight, E. V., *The Bible and the Reader: An Introduction to Literary Criticism* (Philadelphia: Fortress Press, 1985).

Miscall, P. D., *The Workings of Old Testament Narrative* (Chico/Philadelphia: Scholars Press/Fortress Press, 1983).

Newman, B. M., "Discourse Structure" in *Interpreter's Dictionary of the Bible, Supplementary Volume*, 237–41.

Peterson, N., *Literary Criticism for New Testament Critics* (Philadelphia: Fortress Press, 1978).

Poland, L. M., *Literary Criticism and Biblical Hermeneutics: A Critique of Formalist Approaches* (Chico: Scholars Press, 1986).

Preminger, A. and E. L. Greenstein (eds.), *The Hebrew Bible in Literary Criticism* (New York: Ungar Publishing Company, 1986).

Ricoeur, P., *The Conflict of Interpretations: Essays in Hermeneutics* (Evanston: Northwestern University Press, 1974).

Ricoeur, P., *Essays on Biblical Interpretation* (Philadelphia: Fortress Press, 1980).

Robertson, D., "Literature, the Bible as" in *Interpreter's Dictionary of the Bible, Supplementary Volume*, 547–51.

Robertson, D., *The Old Testament and the Literary Critic* (Philadelphia: Fortress Press, 1977).

Ryken, L. (ed.), *The New Testament in Literary Criticism* (New York: Ungar Publishing Company, 1984).

Sternberg, M., *The Poetics of Biblical Narrative* (Bloomington: Indiana University Press, 1985).

Rhetorical Analysis

Betz, H. D., *Galatians: A Commentary on Paul's Letter to the Churches in Galatia* (Philadelphia: Fortress Press, 1979).

Clines, D. J. A. et al. (eds.), *Art and Meaning: Rhetoric in Biblical Literature* (Sheffield: JSOT Press, 1982).

Corbett, E. P. J., *Classical Rhetoric for the Modern Student* (New York/London: Oxford University Press, 1965).

*Gitay, Y., *Prophecy and Persuasion: A Study of Isaiah 40–48* (Bonn: Linguistica Biblica, 1981).

Gitay, Y., "A Study of Amos' Art of Speech: A Rhetorical Analysis of Amos 3:1–15," in *Catholic Biblical Quarterly* 42 (1980) 293–309.

Gitay, Y., "Reflections on the Study of the Prophetic Discourse: The Question of Isaiah I 2–20," in *Vetus Testamentum* 33 (1983) 207–21.

Jackson, J. J. and M. Kessler (eds.), *Rhetorical Criticism: Essays in Honor of James Muilenburg* (Pittsburgh/Edinburgh: Pickwick Press/T. & T. Clark, 1974).

*Kennedy, G. A., *New Testament Interpretation Through Rhetorical Criticism* (Chapel Hill/London: University of North Carolina Press, 1984).

Lyons, G., *Pauline Autobiography: Toward a New Understanding* (Atlanta: Scholars Press, 1985).

Muilenburg, J., "Form Criticism and Beyond" in *Journal of Biblical Literature* 88 (1969) 1–18.

*Wilder, A., *Early Christian Rhetoric: The Language of the Gospel* (London/New York: SCM Press/Harper & Row, 1964; reprinted, Cambridge/London: Harvard University Press, 1971).

*Wuellner, W., "Where is Rhetorical Criticism Taking Us?" *Catholic Biblical Quarterly* 49 (1987) 448–63.

CHAPTER 6

FORM CRITICISM:

The Genre and Life Setting of the Text

Literary criticism, as discussed in the previous chapter, focuses on the "world of the text." In that chapter, we stressed the importance of seeing a text in relation to the larger literary composition in which it is located. Form criticism, or better, genre analysis, though not uninterested in the larger literary blocks of material or even books, focuses more on the smaller literary sections or pericopes. Genre analysis is that aspect of criticism which examines the form, content, and function of a particular unit and asks whether these are definite enough and typical enough for the unit to be classified and interpreted as belonging to a particular genre. If these factors are found to occur in a recognizably similar pattern, and if definite criteria can be established by which one can identify the pattern's occurrence, the unit may be said to belong to a given genre. Knowing the genre of a text allows us to know what types of questions can sensibly be asked of the material.

Form criticism, however, is not concerned merely with identifying various literary genres and then classifying a particular passage within one of these genres, as if defining the genre with its typical features will in some magical sense provide the clue to meaning and interpretation. In addition to genre analysis and classification, form criticism is also concerned with establishing or determining the "situation in life" (*Sitz im Leben*) in which the particular genres were produced, shaped, and used. The phrase "in life" calls attention to the actual "life setting" in which forms of expression arose and were employed. This dimension of form criticism underscores the vital connection between literary genres, their particular institutional and social setting, and their total cultural background.

One benefit of paying closer attention to the genre of texts has been an increased awareness of how directly literary form and content are related to meaning. As we noted earlier, exegesis is an everyday activity in a more general sense, and in everyday exegesis the ordinary person recognizes the relationship between form and content. We recognize that a classified ad in a newspaper belongs to a clearly defined genre with its own set of criteria and expectations. A description of property for sale in a classified ad differs radically from a description of the same property in a deed. One is an advertisement designed to sell the property; the other is a legal description designed to record accurately what has been sold. Every person recognizes that a certain amount of hyperbole and overstatement is allowed, even expected, in the former but not in the latter. Consquently, we read them with different expectations and we interpret them differently. How we understand the description of the property, in other words, is directly related to the literary genre in which the description occurs.

To extend the illustration, the modern reader also recognizes, although perhaps only tacitly, the importance of "setting in life" in interpreting a document. The life setting of a newspaper advertisement is far different from that of a legal document bound and shelved in a government complex. The life setting of advertising and selling property creates a situation which emphasizes the positive features while deemphasizing or even ignoring the negative features. Exaggeration is a built-in ingredient of the life setting of advertising and selling and because we all know this we tend to allow for this as we interpret advertisements and sales pitches. In everyday exegesis, therefore, we recognize the interconnectedness of what is said (content), how it is said (form), and in what setting it is said (setting in life), and we integrate all three as we understand and interpret all sorts of statements.

Form criticism of biblical texts operates with a similar set of perspectives. The exegete who is attentive to form critical concerns makes several distinct interpretive moves. In trying to understand the content of a biblical passage, or what is said in the passage, the interpreter should be alert to its genre and literary structure or how the content is arranged and stated. Once this is done, we then try to determine the life setting or the actual situation(s) in which such a text originated and developed. If we can determine this, we then try to ascertain how the text functioned in that setting. All of this in turn assists us in gaining competence in reading and understanding the content.

These two dimensions of form criticism—the classification of biblical material into various genres and the association of these genres with sociological realities in the life of ancient Israel and the early church—

have been increasingly recognized within the past century or so of biblical scholarship. In the nineteenth century, investigations of the biblical text tended to focus on historical, documentary, and literary questions in a different sense. Historical criticism had come to recognize that many biblical writings "grew" out of certain historical contexts over periods of time. Literary and documentary criticism sought especially to detect various sources upon which the final form of the biblical texts was based. These approaches, however, showed little concern for the individual literary units and specific genres within the biblical text or for the sociological soil—those typical occasions of human existence—in which they were rooted and had grown. These came into prominence as scholars sought to go beyond documentary and historical analysis in order to gain an empathetic appreciation of how the biblical materials had been utilized in ancient cultures before they became fixed in writing.

The book of Psalms proved to be one of the first blocks of biblical material to be analyzed profitably from form-critical perspectives. Consequently, the psalms came to be classified into distinct literary genres: laments (both individual and communal), thanksgivings (both individual and communal), and hymns. Other genres were also identified, but perhaps most significant was the recognition that each of the broad types of psalms followed fairly clearly definable patterns of content, mood, and structure. Equally important was the recognition that the psalms, far from being a collection of hymns, poems, and odes written by a single figure, such as David, were produced within the community of Israel to express and address its various and recurring needs. The majority of them came to be seen as the liturgical texts used in Israelite services of worship. The psalter was now seen as the song and prayer book of ancient Israel reflecting the richness and diversity of the people's life, especially its life of worship. The psalms could no longer be read as if they were part of a single genre, "the book of Psalms," for they were now seen to be connected integrally with many "life settings" within the community and worship of Israel. They not only gave expression to Israel's faith but also reflected that faith and the life which supported it. In this way, form-critical analysis of the psalms made it possible to see how integrally connected are the literary, historical, and sociological dimensions of these biblical texts.

Just as the psalms "came to life" through form-critical investigations, so did other parts of the biblical text when they were examined in similar fashion. The narratives in Genesis were no longer explored merely to ascertain their documentary sources or their historical value but were viewed as "stories" arising out of and expressing the folk life of the people. Prophetic books, too, could no longer be read "on the flat," for they were seen to contain numerous smaller literary units, each quite often reflective of different life settings. It became necessary for the interpreter to be more refined in interpreting the prophetic material. One now had to ask more than simply whether a text was a "prophetic address," but what type of prophetic address—judgment, promise, admonition, exhortation, or what?

The New Testament writings, first the Gospels and later the letters, came to be investigated from a similar perspective. Investigations of the Gospels uncovered numerous smaller genres, such as miracle stories, pronouncement stories, parables, birth stories, to mention only a few. The epistles also revealed a wide variety of smaller genres, such as hymns, prayers of various sorts, kerygmatic or sermon outlines, and confessions. The impact on our understanding of the New Testament was as dramatic as had been the case with the Old Testament. The faith and life of the early church came to light in a new way and many dimensions of that faith and life became visible in an unprecedented fashion. The New Testament writings were seen as literary productions within which the reader could now hear early Christians worshiping (praying and singing), preaching, teaching, confessing, and defending their faith.

If historical criticism succeeds in uncovering the history of the documents and in allowing us to see their "linear life," form criticism succeeds in pointing to the sociological and liturgical dimensions underneath individual texts and allows us to see their "vertical life." The biblical writings, it was discovered, had both historical breadth and sociological depth. A given text might be one step or link within a continuous history, but it might just as well be the proverbial tip of a historical and sociological iceberg, with a substructural history and life of its own.

To be more specific, when form-critical analysis is applied to a royal enthronement psalm, such as Psalm 2, it is as concerned with the "life setting" reflected within the psalm as it is with what is being stated within the psalm. The coronation of a king within ancient Israel is seen to have been the likely setting for which this psalm was originally formulated and in which it came to be repeated on successive occasions. Consequently, the interpreter wonders less about the explicit identity of who is being referred to or who speaks in the psalm as the "king" and "the Lord's anointed." Indeed, as it turns out, what is said in the psalm, its content, is seen to be integrally related to the life setting which gave it birth, and the clue to understanding both is being able to recognize and appreciate its genre. Thus, form, content, life setting, and function are all interrelated and inform each other in the act of form-critical interpretation.

A miracle story from the Gospels such as the healing of the Gerasene demoniac (see Mark 5:1–20 and parallels), to take an example from the New Testament, is one episode within the overall Gospel story. We may study the narrative as depicting an event within the life of Jesus' own ministry and interpret it with a recognition of the historical setting and how this event is reported in each of the Gospels. Consequently, we take into as full account as possible the historical and social setting of the life and ministry of Jesus in analyzing the story. Accordingly, we seek to understand demon possession within first-century Palestine, how it was conceived and understood, but also the role of Jesus in the episode. Consideration may be given to how each Gospel writer used the story. At this level, the interpreter is still attempting to reconstruct the event which may have given birth to the story and to explore how each of the evangelists has employed the story.

A new dimension enters the picture when the same story is considered form-critically. Form-critical analysis of this text would begin by identifying its literary genre as a "miracle story," more specifically an exorcism. Having determined its literary form, we would then note the formal elements in the story, or its literary structure, such as the description of the demon-possessed man (verses 2–5), his encounter with Jesus the miracle-worker (verses 6–10), a description of the healing miracle itself (verses 11–13), the aftermath, including the impact on the crowds and a description of the healed man (verses 14–20). By analyzing the formal structure of similar miracle stories, both biblical and non-biblical, we can determine that the story exhibits a typical pattern seen in other ancient miracle stories. Once we determine this formal outline, it is possible to see how the parallel accounts in Matthew (8:28–34) and Luke (8:26–39) have either expanded or compressed certain formal features.

Besides identifying the genre of the text and analyzing its formal structure, form-critical analysis also inquires into the so-called "oral period," the time between the "original occurrence" of the episode within the life of Jesus and the time when the story was incorporated into the final form of the gospel writing. Form criticism recognizes that during this time, this story like many other such stories circulated orally within the early church. As they were told and retold in the various life settings of preaching, teaching, and worship, they acquired a certain shape to fit the setting. Within these settings, such stories as Mark 5:1–20 acquired their present form and content, being shaped by the Christian community for its own uses.

With its recognition of the oral, preliterary period in which many of the stories about Jesus circulated, form criticism enables us to account for variations within the same story as reported in two or more Gospels. As long as interpreters worked at the literary and historical levels exclusively, it was difficult to provide a satisfactory explanation of the differences in the content and arrangement of certain episodes and teachings in the Gospels. For example, the healing of the Gerasene demoniac exhibits intriguing variations in each of the synoptic accounts. In Matthew's account, there are *two* demoniacs, whereas in Mark and Luke there is only one. Mark records the number of swine as "about two thousand," whereas Matthew and Luke omit this fantastic detail. Such variations are more easily accounted for when we recognize that the same story was told and retold numerous times on various occasions and in different settings. In this way, we see that Matthew records one version of the story as it was told in the early church, whereas Mark and Luke preserve another version of the same story.

Besides helping us to explain many of the differences we find in various accounts of the same story or saying, form-critical analysis also makes it possible to determine the ways in which the story has been shaped, or edited, in the final stage of writing. This allows us to see that the text, even in its final literary form, also possesses another "life setting," that of the author/compiler. In many instances, it is clear that this setting differs quite significantly from earlier settings in which the story or saying was used. This final "setting in life" obviously must take into account the author's own historical, geographical, and social setting, but also his literary purposes and theological interests as well. This will be discussed further in the chapter on redaction criticism, which deals more thoroughly, and intentionally, with the final form of the text and the author's literary and theological purposes.

Form-critical analysis has been especially useful in investigating and interpreting the parables of Jesus. At one time, the parables as a whole were read as if they belonged to the single genre "allegory." Form-critical analysis has enabled us not only to see that there are different types of parables, such as parables of judgment or parables of the kingdom, but that their formal structure as well as their content often provide clues to their original life setting. Consequently, when we read the parables form-critically, we try to reconstruct the various settings in which they were used and then determine how they functioned in those settings. Often their placement in the Gospels themselves provides useful clues. For example, the parable of the lost sheep occurs in different contexts in Matthew (18:12–14) and Luke (15:3–7). In the former, it occurs in a context where proper behavior in the church is the main concern, and there it serves to remind us to care for the "little ones," probably meaning recent converts. In the latter, it occurs in a context where Jesus is disputing with Pharisees and scribes about his associating with social outcasts, the tax collectors and sinners. There it is joined with the parable of the lost coin and the parable of the lost son and serves to underscore the inestimable worth of even a single sinner. In one case the setting is catechetical, providing concrete instructions for church conduct. In the other case the setting is one of polemical controversy in which the parable functions for another purpose altogether. It is entirely possible that these two *literary* settings reflect the type of actual life settings in which the parable circulated in the early church.

Form-critical perspectives on a New Testament, especially a Gospel, text thus focus more on the stories as typical forms of expression rather than as narratives or reports about an event in the life of Jesus and seek to determine how these were used in the life of the church and shaped for its purposes. Thus form criticism allows the interpreter to understand and appreciate the role and significance of the faith and practices of the believing community in the formation of the traditions that the community would hold sacred and declare canonical.

Form-critical analysis can, of course, be applied to entire books and certainly is not merely relevant to the oral stage of materials or to their prewritten form. For example, apocalypses, such as the books of Daniel and Revelation belong to a distinct genre. As such, they possess characteristic elements of content, form, and function. Most of the book of Deuteronomy belongs to the genre of "farewell addresses." To speak of the genre of a written work may not mean that the document is devoid of earlier materials or other genres. Apocalyptic literature often contains such genres as "vision reports" which we know from both prophetic and historical literature. Deuteronomy, although a farewell-address genre, incorporates many other genres including various forms of laws.

We should not assume that every text will lend itself to a complete form-critical analysis. Some texts may well be fresh productions in that they have no history prior to the literary setting in which they occur. Their only life setting may be that of the document itself and the situation of the author-audience in which it arose. These texts, which exhibit typical recurrent formal patterns and behind which we can see prior stages are best suitable for form-critical analysis.

Commentaries on biblical books ordinarily provide the reader with genre classifications, but other more specialized studies also provide a more extensive set of categories. The reader, in trying to classify the passage according to genre, should ask what it is: Is it a prophetic call narrative? a prophetic oracle? a proverb? a psalm of lament? a miracle story? a letter? a hymn? and so forth. Even if this preliminary classification is provisional, it is a necessary exegetical step since it allows the interpreter to raise the questions of form and setting. If the text is seen to be in the form of a psalm of communal lament, for example, the interpreter will then need to determine something about its life setting by asking what circumstances could have given rise to such a lament—a defeat in battle, a natural catastrophe, or what, and how such a lament was utilized in a service of worship with its various components. As the answers to such questions become clearer, understanding of the form and the content of the passage and how it is to be "read" and understood also become clearer, because all aspects of genre analysis interact with each other. For example, a psalm may initially be utterly incomprehensible, until one discovers that it is a communal lament sung by the community. The various stanzas, and how they relate to each other, that is, the form and structure will become much clearer, and the interpreter will be able to read the content of the psalm with much greater understanding. In like fashion, study of typical forms and content can lead one to grasp the typical life setting of texts.

BIBLIOGRAPHY

General

Buss, M. J., "The Idea of Sitz-im-Leben—History and Critique" in *Zeitschrift für Alttestamentliche Wissenschaft* 90 (1978) 157–70.

Collins, J. J. (ed.), *Apocalypse: The Morphology of a Genre (Semeia* 14; Missoula: Scholars Press, 1979).

Doty, W. G., "The Concept of Genre in Literary Analysis" in *Society of Biblical Literature Proceedings* (ed. by L. C. McGaughy; Society of Biblical Literature, 1972) 2.413–18.

Greenwood, D., "Rhetorical Criticism and Formgeschichte: Some Methodological Considerations" in *Journal of Biblical Literature* 89 (1970) 418–26.

Hellholm, D., "The Problem of Apocalyptic Genre and the Apocalypse of John" in *Society of Biblical Literature Seminar Papers* (ed. by K. H. Richards; Chico: Scholars Press, 1982).

*Lohfink, G., *The Bible: Now I Get It! A Form Criticism Handbook* (Garden City: Doubleday & Company, 1979).

Knight, D. A., "The Understanding of 'Sitz im Leben' in Form Criticism" in *Society of Biblical Literature Seminar Papers* (ed. by P. A. Achtemeier; Missoula: Society of Biblical Literature, 1974) 1.105–25.

*Koch, K., *The Growth of the Biblical Tradition* (London/New York: A. & C. Black/Charles Scribner's Sons, 1969).

Old Testament Form Criticism

Gunkel, H., "Fundamental Problems of Hebrew Literary History" in his *What Remains of the Old Testament and Other Essays* (New York/London: Macmillan Company/Allen and Unwin, 1928) 57–68.

Hayes, J. H. (ed.), *Old Testament Form Criticism* (San Antonio: Trinity University Press, 1974).

Knierim, R., "Old Testament Form Criticism Reconsidered" in *Interpretation* 27 (1973) 435–68.

Knierim, R. and G. M. Tucker (eds.), *The Forms of the Old Testament Literature* (24 vols.; Grand Rapids: Eerdmans Publishing Company, 1981–).

*Tucker, G. M., *Form Criticism of the Old Testament* (Philadelphia: Fortress Press, 1971).

Tucker, G. M., "Form Criticism, OT" in *Interpreter's Dictionary of the Bible, Supplementary Volume.* 342–45.

New Testament Form Criticism

Bultmann, R., *The History of the Synoptic Tradition* (rev. ed.; Oxford/New York: Basil Blackwell/Harper & Row, 1968).

*Bultmann R. and K. Kundsin, *Form Criticism: Two Essays on New Testament Research* (Chicago/New York: Willett, Clark and Company/Harper Torchbooks, 1934/1962).

Carlston, C. E., "Form Criticism, NT" in *Interpreter's Dictionary of the Bible, Supplementary Volume*, 345–48.

Dahl, N. A., "Letter" in *Interpreter's Dictionary of the Bible, Supplementary Volume*, 538–41.

Dibelius, M., *From Tradition to Gospel* (London/New York: James Clarke & Co. Ltd/Charles Scribners's Sons, 1934/1965).

Doty, W. G., "The Discipline and Literature of New Testament Form Criticism" in *Anglican Theological Review* 51 (1969) 257–321.

Ellis, E. E., "New Directions in Form Criticism" in *Jesus Christus in Historie und Theologie* (ed. by G. Strecker; Tübingen: J. C. B. Mohr [Paul Siebeck], 1975) 299–315.

*McKnight, E. V., *What Is Form Criticism?* (Philadelphia: Fortress Press, 1969).

Riesenfeld, H., *The Gospel Tradition and Its Beginnings: A Study in the Limits of "Formgeschichte"* (London: A. R. Mowbray and Co., 1957).

Stanton, G., "Form Criticism Revisited" in *What About the New Testament?* (ed. by M. Hooker and C. Hickling; London: SCM Press, 1975) 13–27.

Taylor, V., *The Formation of the Gospel Tradition* (London: Macmillan and Co., 1933).

CHAPTER 7

TRADITION CRITICISM:

The Stages Behind the Text

All cultures have traditions which one generation passes on to the next. Such traditions give expression to peoples' self-understanding, their sense of their past, their systems of belief, and their codes of conduct. Sub-groups within the larger whole may have their own special traditions. These traditions are passed down in the form of stories, sayings, songs, poems, confessions, creeds, and so on. Tradition criticism is concerned with both the nature of these traditions and how they are employed and modified in the course of a community's history.

Much of the Bible is composed of such traditions and reflects the crystallization of the traditions at a particular stage. In fact, different stages of the same tradition may have crystallized at different places and in different ways within the text. These different stages may be reflective of different chronological periods or different theological perspectives or both. (Within Judaism and Christianity, certain interpretations of biblical traditions, of course, have themselves become "traditions.")

Not every biblical text passed through stages of growth and development prior to its appearance in a biblical book, but many did. In those instances where this is clearly the case, tradition criticism offers a valuable perspective and a useful set of methodological approaches for looking at a biblical text.

Within the last two hundred years of biblical scholarship, it has been increasingly recognized that many parts of the Bible "grew" over long periods of time. In some instances this growth occurred over a period of decades, in other instances over centuries. The Old Testament reflects this type of organic development in many of its parts, but the Pentateuch provides perhaps the best example of a part of the Bible which has been formed over a long period of time. It is now widely regarded as a work which reflects multiple editorial activities and diverse chronological periods. Based on distinctive literary characteristics, such as language and style, as well as on theological perspectives discernible within the text, layers, strata, or sources have been discovered in the Pentateuch. These layers have been designated J, E, D, and P. Much of the New Testament, though composed over a much shorter span of time than the Old Testament, reflects a similar period of growth and development prior to the actual writing of the documents themselves. This is especially the case with the Gospels.

In both the Old and New Testaments, therefore, a period prior to the final literary stage of the biblical documents can be recognized. This period has come to be frequently designated the "oral period," because it is assumed to be a time in which the stories and other traditions which later came to be codified within the text circulated in unwritten form, being used and re-used within the communities of Israel and the church respectively. As they were preserved and transmitted, they took on the quality of "traditions," that is, they were thought to be valuable enough, indeed sacred enough, to be passed on from generation to generation. The term tradition, after all, simply refers to that which has been handed over, or passed along, whether sacred or not, but in the context of the Old or New Testament, it obviously denotes those stories and materials which the communities of faith regarded as sacred and normative in defining their faith and practice.

Tradition criticism, however, need not be confined to an "oral period." Traditions may be either written or oral or both. Even if a sacred tradition or story at first circulated in an oral form and was transmitted orally through several generations, after it came to be recorded it still partook of the nature of tradition. It only changed with respect to the manner in which it was handed on. The "traditioning" process thus may involve both oral and written traditions. In either case, tradition criticism is concerned with that aspect of biblical writings where growth and development have occurred. In some instances, certain biblical texts have no pre-history. They appear to have been composed by a single individual at a single point in time for a specific situation. They did not exist prior to that moment in any "pre-packaged" form, and they only exhibit the features of previous traditions to the extent that they draw in a general way on the ethos and atmosphere of the sacred communities or utilize traditional themes, patterns, or plot motifs.

In other cases, however, certain biblical texts show clear signs of growth and development. They resemble geological formations where later layers can be distinguished from earlier layers. When this is the case, the interpreter's task is, first, to detect these layers of literary formation, and second, having done so, to determine how this has occurred and why. Above all, the interpreter engages in this tradition-critical analysis in order to understand better the final form of the text, or the text which one reads in the Bible itself.

Before looking at specific biblical examples, we should note that the process of growth and development of traditions presupposed by tradition criticism can be seen in numerous modern instances which illustrate the way in which traditional materials grow and develop. Quite frequently, one encounters different versions of the same hymn in various denominational hymnbooks. Some versions have three verses, while others might have five or six. Even the same verse may show slightly different wording from hymnbook to hymnbook. If one is trying to understand a particular version of a hymn, certain questions become obvious: Is this the original version of the hymn? Or, was there even an original version? Is this version an earlier or a later version? Is the author whose name appears at the top of the hymn responsible for it, in whole or only in part? How does this compare with a shorter version of the hymn in another hymnbook? Is the shorter version an earlier version which was expanded later, or is it a shortened form of a longer version? In such a case it becomes clear that the hymn has been "traditioned." It has originated at some point, been transmitted and modified until it now can be found in various forms.

It should also be noted that various changes one might detect within the hymn might bear further investigation. The recent concern to make the language of worship more inclusive by eliminating sexist language from many traditional hymns has resulted in numerous revisions, and such changes reflect both historical and sociological, as well as theological, interests. These concrete changes in the tradition may then be related directly to specific settings in life, and the wording of the hymn may be difficult to comprehend otherwise.

If we take the illustration a step further, suppose we find the hymn, not in a hymnal, but quoted in a sermon or an article. This would represent yet another stage in the development of the tradition, for now the actual literary setting has shifted; the literary context of the hymn is no longer "hymnbook" but "sermon." And, if the hymn is cited in order to make a theological point, or to illustrate some moral lesson, its function has also changed. If the exegete is interpreting the sermon, in the first instance, and not the hymn, then the interpretive process is extended even further. It now becomes possible to recognize (a) that a hymn is being quoted which was produced prior to the sermon itself; it had a pre-history, as it were; (b) that a particular version of the hymn is being cited, and that it differs from other versions one knows or had discovered in other hymnbooks; and (c) that the final form of the hymn quoted in the sermon is best understood in light of the other versions that exist, and that this form will be especially illuminated if one were able to sketch in correct historical sequence how and why the hymn developed to the final form one confronts within the sermon being interpreted.

The biblical writings quite often reflect similar stages of growth which lie behind a particular text. Suppose, for example, one were interpreting the Old Testament injunction to observe the sabbath as recorded in Exodus 20:8–11. After examining the passage and noting its content and structure, one would soon discover another version in Deuteronomy 5:12–15, and more importantly that it differed in several respects. Among other things, one would quickly notice that the Exodus version is shorter by several lines. Second, with respect to the content, one would notice that the primary reason for keeping the sabbath is different in each case. In Deuteronomy, observance of the sabbath is grounded in the exodus deliverence, while in Exodus it is related to the creation of the world. Further investigation would uncover other instances in the Old Testament where brief, unelaborated injunctions to keep the sabbath occur (Leviticus 19:3).

Fairly obvious questions would occur to the interpreter at this point: How do the two versions of the same commandment in the Decalogue relate to each other? Is the shorter earlier than the longer, or is it an abbreviated later version? What accounts for the two different theological rationales which are adduced for keeping the sabbath? Were there originally two, each of which was preserved in an independent form? Or, were there originally two different settings out of which these two versions arose, each representing a different theological perspective? How are these elaborated forms of the sabbath ordinance related to the unelaborated or other forms? These are the questions tradition criticism would ask, but it would go further. It would recognize that both versions of the same commandment represent the final literary form of a lengthy process of formation and development, and based on observations of content, structure, and setting, that is, on form-critical observations, would seek to reconstruct how the tradition of the sabbath-observance injunction developed. Having reconstructed this "history of tradition," the exegete would then come back to the final form of the text in Exodus 20, since this was the original point of departure, and propose an explanation interpreting this particular form, and in addition, doing so in light of its immediate literary context.

Many of the narratives of the Pentateuch have been analyzed in terms of the history of tradition. If one assumes that these narratives existed originally as independent, self-contained units then it is possible to sense some of the stages through which they developed. The figure of Jacob, for example, appears to have been initially a trickster-type character who succeeded by outmaneuvering other figures (Esau and Laban). At this level of the tradition, one would have had folktales of a type common to many cultures. When Jacob came to be identified in the stories with the community Israel and his victims with other groups (Esau = Edomites; Laban = Arameans), the tales took on a nationalistic coloration reflecting historical relationships (note that the prophet Hosea shows familiarity with and uses some of these traditions; Hosea 12). When combined with comparable traditions about Abraham, Isaac, and the tribes of Israel, the Jacob stories moved toward being part of a large theological-historical portrait of the origin and history of Israel.

One of the most widespread traditions in the Old Testament concerns the redemption from Egypt. The exodus motif and the tradition of being led out of Egypt occur in Old Testament narratives, psalms, and prophetical books. It was a tradition that could be used in various contexts—in Hosea the ruin of the nation is depicted as a return to Egypt whereas Isaiah 40—55 presents the return from exile as a new exodus.

The fullest expanded tradition in the Pentateuch is that of the wilderness, now extending from Exodus 15:22 through Deuteronomy 34. Frequently, in credal-life summaries of Israel's early tradition, the wilderness is not mentioned (see Deuteronomy 26:5–11) or else only occurs incidentally (see Joshua 24:7b). This tradition of the stay in the wilderness was developed in various ways in ancient Israel—as a time of trouble and wickedness (in most of Exodus—Numbers, Exekiel 20) or as a good time (Deuteronomy 8; 29:2–6; Jeremiah 2:2–3; Hosea 2:14–15). This twofold development and utilization of a tradition can be seen in a comparison of Psalms 105 and 106.

Within many of the historical books, the traditions about the election and choice of David, his dynasty, and his city—Zion-Jerusalem—dominate (1 and 2 Samuel; 1 and 2 Chronicles). These same traditions are integral to many psalms.

Time and again, Israel gave expression to its self-understanding and its hopes for the future by reusing and dialoguing with its traditions. When exegeting a passage influenced by or reflecting such traditions, the interpreter can learn much from an understanding of how these traditions developed and were used.

From the New Testament, numerous examples could be adduced from the Gospels to illustrate the importance of understanding the history of traditions, but a clear example is provided by the Pauline writings. In 1 Corinthians 15:1–11, Paul recites a summary of the message which he had preached to the Corinthians on his initial missionary stay. It is now widely agreed among scholars that verses 3–5 consist of a pre-Pauline summary of Chritian preaching, at least one version of it. This has been established by noting that Paul refers to delivering what he had received as well as by noting the terms within this summary that are either unusual for Paul or not used by him elsewhere in his writings. The summary has a four-part structure: Christ (a) died, (b) was buried, (c) was raised, and (d) appeared. What we have here is clearly a pre-Pauline summary of the early Christian preaching which he has quoted and incorporated into this letter. He is not the author of it, only its transmitter or "traditioner." Further examination of verses 6–11 reveal that at some point Paul ceases to quote this earlier tradition and begins to speak his own sentiments. Exactly where this happens, whether at verse 6 or verse 7, is not clear, but certainly by the time the paragraph ends, we hear Paul himself speaking, not the tradition.

Operating from the perspective of tradition criticism, the exegete would first detect this "layered" quality of 1 Corinthians 15:1–11, and isolate those portions where the tradition is speaking, and separate them from the portions where Paul is speaking. Having done so, the exegete would then examine other summary outlines of the early Christian preaching, such as those in the speeches in Acts, and other places, to determine what state in the history of the tradition of this kerygmatic summary 1 Corinthians 15:3–6 belongs. Is it an extended form of the two-part summaries like one finds in Romans 8:34, or are the latter an abbreviated form? Is it earlier or later than other such summaries? How does it compare with later summary outlines of early Christian preaching, or confessions say from the late first or early second century, such as the Apostle's Creed? All of these questions, properly answered, would have the effect of sharpening one's understanding of 1 Corinthians 15:3–6. To the degree that the exegete can reconstruct the history of tradition, both prior to and after the text being studied, to that degree tradition criticism will illuminate the exegesis of the text.

After examining the final form of the tradition, that is, Paul's quotation of it in 1 Corinthians, the exegete is then prepared to interpret Paul's use of it. Here one would seek to determine precisely where the tradition ceases and where Paul's own remarks begin. Then one would seek to determine the precise ways Paul himself interprets this tradition. Further discussion of this aspect of the text will occur in the following chapter on redaction criticism.

Tradition criticism points up an important dimension of the biblical writings which we have alluded to earlier, namely their cumulative growth, but more specifically that the biblical writings in many instances have actually taken up and incorporated earlier traditions into the biblical text itself. The biblical writings, on this showing, are seen to reflect the traditioning process, and interpreters, both ancient and modern, who confront the biblical text participate in a similar activity. What repeatedly occurs in both the Old and New Testament is something like the following: an interpreter, whether an individual or a community, inherits a sacred tradition, either oral or written, "receives the tradition" to use the technical term, repeats and interprets this tradition in light of the interpreter's own current situation, and then having done so, transmits this interpreted tradition to successors. The biblical writings both receive and interpret earlier sacred traditions, but they have also *become* sacred traditions, used and transmitted by the two communities of faith, Israel and the church. What they record attests the various aspects of the faith and life of both Israel and the church, and quite often how Israel and the church have participated in this process of transmission is as vital to understanding the final form of the written text as anything else. It is this dimension of the text which tradition criticism addresses.

It should be clear how dependent tradition criticism is on the previous exegetical techniques we have discussed. Quite obviously, form-critical observations are required before one can attempt to reconstruct the stages of development behind a text. Similarly, one must be attentive to both historical and literary dimensions within the text. Even textual criticism sometimes plays a vital role in establishing the history of the tradition. Tradition criticism, then, must be done in close concert with other exegetical disciplines, but in spite of its close connection with them, it nevertheless constitutes a separate discipline.

The hypothetical nature of the tradition-critical task should also be noted. Those scholars who emphasize this particular exegetical discipline are the first to acknowledge how theoretical and hypothetical is the process of reconstructing the previous history of a text by isolating distinctive forms of the text, arranging them in chronological sequence, and assessing various aspects of the stages of development. To be sure, in some instances, this can be done with relative certainty and with a high degree of confidence; in other instances, the level of probability shades off into only possibility, perhaps even into unlikelihood. In any case, all of these reconstructive efforts are made with a view to explicating and illuminating the final form of the written text which confronts the exegete on the pages of the Bible itself. The final form of the text, then, functions as the final norm and control for all tradition-critical investigation.

BIBLIOGRAPHY

General

Lord, A. B., *The Singer of Tales* (Cambridge/London: Harvard University Press, 1964).

Olrich, A., "Epic Laws of Folk Narrative," in *The Study of Folklore* (ed. by A. Dundes; Englewood Cliffs: Prentice-Hall, 1965) 129–41.

Pelikan, J., *The Vindication of Tradition* (New Haven/London: Yale University Press, 1984).

Shils, E., *Tradition* (Chicago: University of Chicago Press, 1981).

Vansina, J., *Oral Tradition: A Study in Historical Methodology* (London: Routledge and Kegan Paul, 1965).

Old Testament Tradition Criticism

Coats, G. W., "Tradition Criticism, OT" in *Interpreter's Dictionary of the Bible, Supplementary Volume*, 912–14.

Culley, R. C. (ed.), *Oral Tradition and Old Testament Studies (Semeia 5*; Missoula: Scholars Press, 1976).

Gunkel, H., *The Legends of Genesis: The Biblical Saga and History* (Chicago: Open Court, 1901; reprinted, New York: Schocken Books, 1964).

Gunkel, H., "Jacob" in his *What Remains of the Old Testament and Other Essays* (New York/London: Macmillan Company/Allen and Unwin, 1928) 151–86.

Jeppesen, K. and B. Otzen (eds.), *The Productions of Time: Tradition in Old Testament Scholarship* (Sheffield: Almond Press, 1984).

Knight, D. A., *Rediscovering the Traditions of Israel* (2d ed,; Missoula: Scholars Press, 1975).

*Knight, D. A. (ed.), *Tradition and Theology in the Old Testament* (Philadelphia: Fortress Press, 1977).

Mowinckel, S., "Tradition, Oral" in *Interpreter's Dictionary of the Bible*, 4. 683–85.

Mowinckel, S., *Prophecy and Tradition: The Prophetic Books in the Light of the Study of the Growth and History of the Tradition* (Oslo: J. Dybwad, 1946).

*Nielson, E., *Oral Tradition: A Modern Problem in Old Testament Interpretation* (London: SCM Press, 1954).

Noth, M., *A History of Pentateuchal Traditions* (Englewood Cliffs/Chico: Prentice-Hall/Scholars Press, 1972/1981).

Ohler, A., *Studying the Old Testament: From Tradition to Canon* (Edinburgh: T. & T. Clark, 1985).

von Rad, G., *The Problem of the Hexateuch and Other Essays* (Edinburgh/New York: Oliver & Boyd/McGraw-Hill, 1966).

Rast, W., *Tradition History and the Old Testament* (Philadelphia: Fortress Press, 1972).

New Testament Tradition Criticism

*Barbour, R. S., *Tradition-Historical Criticism of the Gospels* (London: SPCK, 1972).

Calvert, D. G. A., "An Examination of the Criteria for Distinguishing the Authentic Words of Jesus" in *New Testament Studies* 18 (1971–1972) 209–19.

*Catchpole, D. R., "Tradition History" in *New Testament Interpretation: Essays on Principles and Methods* (ed. by I. H. Marshall; Exeter/Grand Rapids: Paternoster Press/Eerdmans Publishing Company, 1977) 165–80.

Cullmann, O., "The Tradition" in his *The Early Church* (London/Philadelphia: SCM Press/Westminster Press, 1956) 59–99.

Gerhardsson, B., *Memory and Manuscript: Oral Tradition and Written Transmission in Rabbinic Judaism and Early Christianity* (Lund: C. W. K. Gleerup, 1961).

Hahn, F., *The Titles of Jesus in Christology: Their History in Early Christianity* (London/New York: Lutterworth Press/World Publishing Co., 1969).

Hooker, M. D., "Christology and Methodology" in *New Testament Studies* 17 (1970–1971) 480–87.

Perrin, N., *Rediscovering the Teaching of Jesus* (London/New York: SCM Press/Harper & Row, 1967).

CHAPTER 8

REDACTION CRITICISM:

The Final
Viewpoint and Theology

As used in biblical exegesis, redaction criticism refers to that form of interpretation whose primary focus is the editorial stage(s) that led toward or produced the final written form or composition of a passage, the final stage(s) of the tradition, as it were, that has become crystallized in written form.

This may appear strange to the beginning exegete who sees this as fairly self-evident. Is not the exegete's task to interpret the text as it lies open before the reader waiting to be understood? Is it not the final written form, and not some earlier draft of a passage which after all has been canonized and calls for interpretation? Has not interpretation of the final text always been the basic concern?

To put the exegete's task this way does make redaction criticism appear to be doing the obvious. This would be the case if other considerations were not in the picture. Redaction criticism presupposes the insights and perspectives of tradition criticism and form criticism. One of its basic operating assumptions is that many biblical texts have a pre-history and that this pre-history can be detected and reconstructed in many instances with a reliable degree of certainty. Moreover, it draws on the findings of these other disciplines which have detected and demonstrated the various ways in which a given story or tradition changes as it is transmitted from person to person or from generation to generation or from one documentary form to another. Given these changes in the form, content, and function of materials the interpreter is concerned not only to pinpoint such changes but to account for them. Even more, the sensitive interpreter wants to know how these changes affect and illuminate the meaning of the story or tradition in its latest form or version.

Another way of making the same point is to observe that some biblical texts do not readily lend themselves to redaction-critical analysis. If it is impossible for the interpreter to detect previous traditions underlying a text, or if a text appears not to be taking up a previous biblical tradition or text and reinterpreting it, in these instances, try as one may, one cannot demonstrate that an author or editor has redacted anything. At the most, one can only posit that the text has been written by an author, not inherited, interpreted, and transmitted in a modified form.

In those instances where a given text clearly reflects the use of previous traditions, texts, or stories, redaction criticism can be a valuable exegetical discipline. The Gospels provide some of the best examples of such instances, because here, quite often, the same event, episode, or saying is reported, even in two, three, or four different versions. In addition, Gospel criticism has made it possible to place the four Gospels along a historical continuum. Although there will never be universal agreement that Mark was the earliest Gospel, and that both Matthew and Luke used the Gospel of Mark as one of their sources, this theory explains the evidence as well as any other, and in the opinion of the majority of scholars, better than any other.

Given these assumptions, one can examine a story or saying of Jesus in Mark, let us say, then examine the same story in either Matthew and Luke, and on the basis of these investigations pinpoint the precise ways in which they have redacted Mark's version of the story. One of the indispensable tools for doing redaction criticism of the Gospels is a synopsis. Several good synopses are readily available, but they all have one thing in common: they arrange the accounts of the Synoptic Gospels (in other instances all four Gospels) in parallel columns, making it possible for the reader to compare the various versions of an episode or teaching, noting both differences and similarities. The synopsis should not be confused with another exegetical tool, the harmony, even though both types of work are arranged in similar fashion. Unlike a synopsis, a harmony of the Gospels seeks to harmonize the various stories into a single, coherent story. The attempt is to produce a single Gospel, as it were. A synopsis, by contrast, makes no conscious attempt to harmonize the Gospels nor to underscore the differences for that matter. It is so constructed, taking seriously the indisputable fact that in the New Testament canon we have four Gospels not one, as to lay these accounts side by side, making it possible for the reader to see them together. The term "synopsis " itself means "seeing together."

The one part of all four Gospels which exhibits the greatest uniformity is the Passion Narrative, the account of the final days of Jesus. Here, perhaps better than anywhere else, it becomes indisputably clear that Matthew and Luke have followed Mark, using his account of the passion as their basic outline. Consequently, one can establish the history of the tradition in at least two stages with respect to almost every episode. Once this is done, redaction criticism then seeks to interpret an episode in Matthew or Luke in light of the way they have edited or redacted Mark.

The scene describing Jesus' death on the cross (Matthew 27:45–56; Mark 15:33–41; Luke 23:44–49; see John 19:17–37) may serve as an example. Reading each of the accounts carefully, the interpreter notes that each account has its own distinctive profile. None of the three, in fact, is identical. Matthew's account is longer than Mark's, Luke's is conspicuously shorter. Matthew, therefore, has redacted Mark by expanding it, Luke by abbreviating it. Specific points are also quite different. According to Matthew, after the death of Jesus there occurred, besides the tearing of the temple veil, an earthquake resulting in tombs being opened and saints being resurrected. This occurs in neither Mark nor Luke. Luke, in contrast to Matthew, omits certain features of Mark's account, most notably the cry of dereliction, "My God, my God, why hast thou forsaken me?" Instead of this, he records the final words of Jesus on the cross as being, "Father, into thy hands I commit my spirit!" These last words of Jesus are recorded in none of the other Gospels. Another important difference occurs with respect to the confession of the Roman centurion standing guard at the crucifixion. Matthew follows Mark in recording his confession as "Truly, this was the Son of God!" Luke's account of the confession is completely different: "Certainly this man was innocent!"

Redaction criticism, rather than trying to harmonize these differences into a single story, seeks instead to let each account speak for itself. It also seeks to make sense of the distinctive features of each account in light of two considerations: (a) how the later versions of Matthew and Luke compare with the earlier version of Mark and (b) how the distinctive features of each version relate to the theological perspective and message of the Gospel in which it occurs as a whole.

With respect to the former, a redaction-critical analysis of Luke seeks to explain Luke's omission of the cry of dereliction. It not only makes the comparison with the earlier tradition, but also tries to account for the changes by asking why. Why does Luke omit this cry of dereliction? Because he found it offensive theologically? Because he found it less significant than the more comforting statement, "Father, into thy hands

I commit my spirit"? Similarly, the redaction critic asks why the centurion's confession is worded differently in Luke. Did Luke simply alter the form of the confession which he had before him in Mark? Did he have access to another tradition of the centurion's confession which focused on Jesus' innocence rather than his divinity, and did he choose to record this alternative tradition?

At each stage, the redaction critic, interpreting Luke's account of the death of Jesus on the cross, seeks to interpret the form of the text before the reader, the final written form, over against an earlier written form as seen in Mark. Above all, the redaction critic recognizes a distinction between what is being said *in* the text and what is being said *through* the text. What is being said *in* Luke's version of the death of Jesus is that Jesus died with final words of hope and confidence on his lips, rather than words of desperation, and that the impact of his death on a pagan soldier was to confirm his innocence, nothing else.

What is being said *through* this account can be established by asking whether these particular motifs are recurrent elsewhere in Luke's Gospel. The redaction critic seeks to determine whether Luke's handling of this particular episode is in any sense typical of how he tells the story of Jesus and the church as a whole. In both respects, this turns out to be the case. With respect to the former, the redaction critic discovers that de-emphasizing the agony of the cross and suffering of Jesus is indeed thoroughly typical of Luke's Gospel. To omit the cry of dereliction, it turns out, is completely in keeping with Luke's portrait of Christ throughout his Gospel. The christology of this episode is thoroughly congruent with Luke's christology as a whole.

With respect to the second motif, the innocence of Jesus, the redaction critic examines the rest of the writings of Luke, both the Gospel of Luke and Acts, to determine whether this too is a typical, recurrent theological interest, and this also turns out to be the case. Looking at the immediate literary context, the passion narrative itself, the redaction critic discovers that Luke more than any of the other Gospel writers underscores the innocence of Jesus throughout the passion narrative. He consistently redacts particular episodes in this direction, either by additions, expansions, omissions, or abbreviations (see Luke 23:4, 14–15, 20, 22, 41; also Acts 3:13–14).

What is being said *through* the story turns out to be consistent with other features of Luke's message as a whole: a serious miscarriage of justice was done to Jesus, the innocent prophet, who died confident that he would be vindicated as God's righteous prophet. By noting carefully these distinctive features of Luke's account of the death of Jesus, the redaction critic thus allows the text to speak in its own behalf, concentrating on what is being said *in* the story, but also tries to assess the theological message being articulated in this particular version, trying to ascertain what is being said *through* the story.

In some instances within the Gospels, the interpreter may not be as confident in sketching a history of the tradition behind a text, but it should be noted that establishing a genetic relation between traditions is not always necessary for redaction criticism to occur. For example, if one reads a single story in three or four different versions, even if one cannot place them in a chronological sequence and demonstrate that one has depended on the other, comparing each of the accounts will nevertheless reveal distinctive features of each. Such comparisons, if carried out thoroughly and perceptively, will allow the interpreter to see any given account in much sharper profile. At the very least, then, the interpreter can note these distinctive characteristics, and try to correlate them with similar features within the document as a whole, and thus still try to articulate how they reflect the theological outlook or message of the writer or document. Thus, in one sense, redaction criticism depends heavily on the insights and results of tradition criticism and form criticism, but not in every case.

What is important for the beginning exegete to keep in mind is that the text being studied may exhibit editorial features, clear and distinctive enough to provide important clues leading to a deeper understanding of the passage. Whether these are uncovered by comparing this final version with an earlier version from which it was drawn, or whether these are detected by more general comparisons, either with other biblical versions of the same story, or even with non-biblical versions of a similar story or saying, matters little. What matters is for the interpreter to let the text speak its full message, not a message obscured by reading other versions into it, or by harmonizing other versions with it. This caveat should be taken with full seriousness, because many readers of the Bible have inherited a homogenized, single version of the Gospel story, like Christmas scenes which homogenize Luke's and Matthew's birth stories; this single version succeeds in effectively blocking the message of the individual evangelists.

Redaction criticism, in particular, has called the attention of modern readers to this often obscured aspect of the Gospels, although the ancient titles ascribed to each Gospel in the second and third centuries sought to underscore this distinction. The "Gospel *according* to . . ." was their way of calling attention to the distinctive theological messages of each

Gospel. Consequently, we are now in a much better position to speak of the "theology" of Matthew, even if "Matthew" is now a more shadowy figure than he was once believed to be. Each of the Gospels, to be sure, is anonymous, yet each Gospel reflects a distinctive, definable theological outlook as it seeks to relate the story of Jesus in its own manner.

Redaction criticism served as a healthy corrective to certain trends within both tradition criticism and form criticism as they came to be preoccupied, if not obsessed, with the smaller literary units and sub-units within each Gospel. By contrast, redaction criticism emphasizes the wholeness of the Gospels, their literary integrity, and seeks to see not simply the individual parts, but what they were saying when arranged together as a single whole. Consequently, the redaction critic is never satisfied to analyze a single literary sub-unit or pericope in and of itself, but rather, having done so, to relate it to the larger whole. In this, redaction criticism shares the concern of literary criticism which we discussed earlier, but unlike literary criticism, recognizes the pre-history of the text as noted by form criticism and stresses the theological perspective of the unit in light of the whole.

To this point, our discussion has focused exclusively on New Testament examples, but redaction criticism applies equally well to Old Testament texts. The term "redaction criticism" is used less often, however, in biblical exegesis of Old Testament texts. The term was actually coined by a New Testament scholar in the 1950s, and in this instance, was first emphasized as an exegetical technique in New Testament studies, and later applied to Old Testament studies. The techniques discussed in the previous chapters were almost always developed in exactly the reverse, first being pioneered by Old Testament scholars and later applied and refined by New Testament scholars.

It would be a serious mistake, however, to leave the impression that redaction criticism as an exegetical technique is less than thirty years old. As a matter of fact, biblical scholars have for a long time recognized that the various biblical writings exhibit distinctive theological "tendencies" or portray very clearly defined theological messages. It has also been recognized that these have to be taken into account when reading the biblical documents. It has long been noted that the various editors responsible for the final compilation of the Pentateuch displayed clearly defined theological outlooks and that these were seen to be consistent within certain blocks of material. Similarly, the outlook of the Chronicler has been well known and used to account for the difference in the way certain stories and traditions from Samuel—Kings are interpreted in this work. David, for example, is portrayed in a far more realistic fashion in 1 and 2 Samuel than in 1 Chronicles. The Chronicler reinterpreted these earlier stories and repainted the portrait of David and his time to present both in an idealistic light. The two resulting portraits are noticeably different, a difference that has long been obvious to scholars. Thus, from this perspective, one could say that redaction criticism is not a new methodology but simply a more self-conscious form of an older type of criticism which has developed in light of form and tradition criticisms.

If we take an example of this older form of criticism and contrast this with a redactional-critical perspective, we can see something of the difference resulting from this greater self-consciousness. Scholars have long noted that in 1 Samuel 8—12 there are two basic attitudes (and probably sources) related to the origin of the monarchy. One is pro-monarchy (9:1—10:16; 11:1–15) and the other is anti-monarchy (8:1–22; 10:17–27; 12:1–25). Most older interpreters were content to point out these differences, to work on their possible connections with other sources, and to try to associate the different views with different historical periods or groups. Redaction criticism, however, carries the issues further and asks such questions as: What are the consequences of the manner in which these materials have been redacted in their final form? What significance is there to the fact that the pro-monarchy materials have been "enveloped" and intersected with anti-monarchy materials? From such questions, one can see that obviously the anti-monarchy materials have been given dominance so that the final form of 1 Samuel 8—12 has been redacted to place qualifications on the historical institution of the monarchy. Redaction criticism, however, would further note that 1 Samuel 8—12 forms part of the books of 1 and 2 Samuel and brings this phenomenon into the picture. In 1 Samuel 1:1–10 and 2 Samuel 22:1—23:7, one encounters three poems on kingship which have been redacted into their present location. These poems, again in "envelope" fashion, tend to modify the restrictions placed on kingship in 1 Samuel 8—12 but do so in idealistic and "messianic" terms. In describing the theology of kingship found in 1 and 2 Samuel, all of these, but especially the redactional activity, would need to be considered.

Opportunities to apply redactional perspectives appear throughout the Old Testament. For example, what significance is there to the fact that the Pentateuch (with its laws) ends before the people enter the land? Was the material redacted in this way to stress the torah (the law) as the element constitutive of the society? Was it to address a community in "exile" away from the land? Or to emphasize that obedience to the law is prerequisite to possession of the land? What significance has the redacted form of the prophetical books? What impact does the association of all the material in the book of Isaiah, from such diverse periods, have on the reading of a text in Isaiah?

BIBLIOGRAPHY

Old Testament Redaction Criticism

*Blenkinsopp, J., *Prophecy and Canon: A Contribution to the Study of Jewish Origins* (Notre Dame/London: University of Notre Dame Press, 1977).
Coote, R. B., *Amos Among the Prophets: Composition and Theory* (Philadelphia: Fortress Press, 1981).
March, W. E., "Redaction Criticism and the Formation of Prophetic Books " in *Society of Biblical Literature Seminar Papers* (1977) 87–101.
Mayes, A. D. H., *The Story of Israel Between Settlement and Exile: A Redactional Study of the Deuteronomistic History* (London: SCM Press, 1983).
Nelson, R. D., *The Double Redaction of the Deuteronomistic History* (Sheffield: JSOT Press, 1981).
Noth, M., *The Deuteronomistic History* (Sheffield: JSOT Press, 1981).
Rendsburg, G. A., *The Redaction of Genesis* (Winona Lake, IN: Eisenbrauns, 1985).
*Wharton, J. A., "Redaction Criticism, OT" in *Interpreter's Dictionary of the Bible, Supplementary Volume*, 729–32.

New Testament Redaction Criticism

Bornkamm, G., G. Barth and H. J. Held, *Tradition and Interpretation in Matthew* (London/Philadelphia: SCM Press/Westminster Press, 1963).
Conzelmann, H., *The Theology of St. Luke* (London/New York: Faber and Faber/Harper & Row, 1960/1961).
Fortna, R. T., "Redaction Criticism, NT" in *Interpreter's Dictionary of the Bible, Supplementary Volume*, 733–35.
Lightfoot, R. H., *History and Interpretation in the Gospels* (London/New York: Hodder and Stoughton/Harper & Brothers, 1935).
Marxsen, W., *Mark the Evangelist: Studies on the Redaction History of the Gospel* (Nashville: Abingdon Press, 1969).
*Perrin, N., *What is Redaction Criticism?* (Philadelphia/London: Fortress Press/SPCK, 1969/1970).
*Rohde, J., *Rediscovering the Teaching of the Evangelists* (London/Philadelphia: SCM Press/Westminster Press, 1968).
Stein, R. H., "What is Redaktionsgeschichte?" in *Journal of Biblical Literature* 88 (1969) 45–56.

Representative Biblical Theologies

*Bultmann, R., *Theology of the New Testament* (2 vols.; New York/London: Charles Scribner's Sons/SCM Press, 1951–1955/1952–1955).

Childs, B. S., *Old Testament Theology in a Canonical Context* (London/Philadelphia: SCM Press/Fortress Press, 1985/1986).

Eichrodt, W., *Theology of the Old Testament* (2 vols.; Philadelphia/London: Westminster Press/SCM Press, 1961–1967).

*Goppelt, L., *Theology of the New Testament* (2 vols.; Grand Rapids/London: Eerdmans Publishing Company/SPCK, 1981–1983).

Kümmel, W. G., *The Theology of the New Testament According to Its Major Witnesses: Jesus-Paul-John* (Nashville/London: Abingdon Press/SCM Press, 1973/1976).

Ladd, G. E., *A Theology of the New Testament* (Grand Rapids/London: Eerdmans Publishing Company/Lutterworth Press, 1974/1975).

*von Rad, G., *Old Testament Theology* (2 vols.; Edinburgh/New York: Oliver & Boyd/Harper & Row, 1962–1965).

*Terrien, S. L., *The Elusive Presence: Toward a New Biblical Theology* (San Francisco: Harper & Row, 1978).

CHAPTER 9

STRUCTURALIST CRITICISM:

The Universals in the Text

Most of the methods we have considered in the preceding chapters are primarily historical in orientation. They are employed as an aid in reading and analyzing the text, as the means to understanding the author and the author's thought and intention in terms of the author's time and place or historical context. This is the case even if a text is not considered the product of a particular author but rather the result of a communal effort or process. The goal still remains the same, namely, the desire to understand the text in light of the temporal process or historical/personal developments that produced the text.

In terms of our diagram on page 25, these historical methods focus on (1) the originator of the text, (2) the original audience, and (3) the universe of ideas and events (the historical conditions and circumstances) the two shared. Exegesis is seen as the process through which the reader reads, examines, and listens to the words of the text as a medium communicating the author's message. The text serves as a conduit or vehicle for the author's thought. The exegete asks, "What did the author intend to say to the reader(s) through the text?" The text serves as the means through which the reader understands the author. However much the text lies in the forefront, ultimately the reader's task is to "get through" or "get behind" the text to the author's intended message. The text serves not as an end in itself but the means to a "more important" end—understanding the author and the author's intention. The various forms of historical criticism tend to use the text as a window through which the interpreter looks at other referents (the author, the author's intention, the setting, the context).

Within the last few decades, a method for studying texts in non-historical and atemporal fashion has developed. This approach is "structuralist criticism." The name derives from a methodology developed for analyzing any type of human and social phenomena and activities. Structuralism has been applied in a wide variety of fields including general anthropology, linguistics, and literature.

Several basic assumptions underlie all structuralist studies. Structuralist research assumes that all social activity is governed by abstract conventions, convictions, and rules. These constitute the foundational structures of all cultural systems and manifest themselves in all forms of human social activity. Humans have an innate capacity both for structuring existence and for creating patterns of meaning. Polarities and binary oppositions play important roles in the structuring process. That is, patterns and structures are conceived in such categories as left/right, good/bad, up/down, subject/object, light/darkness, male/female, and so on. These structures need not necessarily be perceived consciously but may function at the unconscious or subconscious level. Some structures and structural patterns are universal and thus are shared across diverse cultural and linguistic boundaries. All social activity, even art and literature, embody and reflect numerous structures. The structural features that are easily perceived are referred to as "surface structures." Speech, for example, reflects certain surface structures that the ordinary person associates with proper use of language and correct grammar and syntax. The use of any language, however, is based also on very complex linguistic structures. Such complex structures are referred to as "deep structures." Thus a person may use and recognize proper speech and be aware of the "surface structures" associated with a language but have no knowledge of the complex grammatical and linguistic structures—the "deep structures"—that underlie the proper use and function of language.

Structuralists assume that literature reflects both surface structures and deep structures. The "deep structures" are reflective of structural patterns that transcend time and space but can be abstracted from specimens of literature. In structuralist interpretation, a text is viewed more as a mirror than as a window. As a mirror, the text reflects universally shared structures and concerns. Thus texts have an integrity of their own apart from the circumstances in which they originated. In structuralist interpretations, a text stands on its own regardless of the text's origins or past and is to be interpreted without concern for the author's assumed original intention. Generic considerations dominate over genetic considerations, not so much because structuralists deny genetic factors but because historical/genetic issues can blur the perception of generic features.

Structuralists are as interested in how texts communicate and have meaning as in what they communicate and mean. They emphasize such questions as the following: How does a particular text produced under particular cultural constraints embody and give expression to universal concerns? How does a reader decode the text or how does the text communicate its deep structure to resonate with the deep structures of the reader? For structural literary critics, emphasis falls on the text and the reader and the process of reading and understanding rather than on such matters as writing and the author's intention.

It is important for us not only to note the differences between structuralist and other kinds of interpretation, but also to understand more fully some of the underlying exegetical assumptions of structuralism. Two major emphases are especially important.

(1) According to structuralist criticism, a text is to be considered *ahistorical* or perhaps more accurately *atemporal*. The structuralist critic reads a text without reference to the element of time; in fact, every effort is made to exclude the dimension of time unless it is a particular concern of the text. This is in sharp contrast to earlier methods we have discussed, where we have come to a text tacitly assuming that we can and should distinguish between an ancient text and a modern reader. This fundamental assumption, which gives rise to efforts to distinguish between what the text meant and what the text means, is simply not a concern of the structuralist critic. Rather, when we read a text, we should assume nothing more than that it exists. In this sense, any text we read is timeless. The text exists in its own right and is to be interpreted on its own terms. Whereas traditional form-criticism, for example, asks questions about origin and original function, structuralism asks questions about the text's underlying assumptions, universal concerns, and its present function in the reader-text relationship.

Those accustomed to interpreting texts according to more traditional methods of exegesis may find this atemporal approach difficult to appreciate, yet it is fundamental in explaining certain basic features of the structuralist critical approach to a biblical text. Two such features should be noted.

First, structuralists are interested only in the final form of the text. It is the text as a finished product that sets the agenda for the structuralist critic. Structuralists have no interest in inquiring into the pre-history of the text, distinguishing between earlier and later forms of the text, or trying to identify parts of the text that might be later interpolations or the work of later redactors or editors. Obviously, structuralist critics recognize that a text may exist in different recensions or versions, as we saw in our dicussion of textual criticism, but this is inconsequential. The basic exegetical move is to accept a text and work with it as a finished piece. How it came to have its present form is immaterial; what is important is what lies before us as a finished work, awaiting interpretation.

Second, the atemporal or timeless view of a text also explains why structuralist critics interpret a text without any reference to its historical setting. Obviously structuralists assume that a text was written by someone, at some time, in some place and setting. But these are of no concern in structuralist criticism. In structuralist criticism, author, original audience, and historical setting are bracketed out. There is no attempt made to answer, or be concerned with, the traditional questions: "Who wrote it?" "To whom was it written?" "When? Where? How? Why?" "Under what circumstances?"

This emphasis on the text itself without regard for its original historical setting means that we must reconstrue how we understand a text to convey meaning. Whatever meaning is being conveyed through the text is not being conveyed from an author through the text, but from the text itself.

This concern for the text in and of itself is described as structuralism's preference for *synchronic* over *diachronic* analysis. Literally, these two frequently used terms mean "with or at the same time" and "through time" respectively. Diachronic analysis presupposes that we can conceive of a text as having existed and developed "through time." It presupposes a historical perspective in which time is a central element. If we do a diachronic word study, for example, we look at such things as etymology, and trace the use of the word, its development and meaning historically, or through time. Diachronic analysis implies a linear model of investigation, one that allows us to chart development and progress along a time line. Synchronic analysis, by contrast, is atemporal or ahistorical and considers a literary work to possess its own meaning. When we compare things synchronically, we do so without any reference to time. For example, if we engage in synchronic analysis of two literary motifs or themes, one from Genesis the other from Acts, we do so not as if one is earlier and one later, but as if they were both "together in time." It has been noted that a better designation than synchronic might be achronic, that is, "without time" or without reference to time.

(2) Structuralist criticism, as we have noted, is based on a view of reality that seeks to understand all forms of human experience and behavior as concrete manifestations of certan ordering principles or

structures that are considered universals. Several things follow from this.

First, the structuralist critic operates with an expanded understanding of the concept "language." Rather than seeing language as communication through words, structuralists understand "language" to include any set of ordered symbols, verbal or non-verbal, through which meaning is conveyed. It is in this sense that they understand all forms of social behavior to reflect underlying "languages" or patterns of language. To the degree that customs of dress are uniform within a given society and conform to well-established, well-accepted rules, we can speak of a "language of dress." The rules governing what to wear and what not to wear, and when to wear it, are comparable to the rules of grammar and syntax that govern what, when, and how we speak or write. We might conceive kinship patterns in a similar fashion. Within a given society, family or tribe, relationships between persons are based on certain established, accepted principles. On the basis of these, persons within a given social group relate to each other and make basic decisions, such as whom they can and cannot marry. In one sense, the persons within this social group may be thought of as the "words" of a language whose arrangement and placement are based on certain principles of "social syntax and grammar."

Second, not only is language understood in a very broad sense, but also the language of any given text is seen to contain varying levels of meanings. Accordingly, structuralists distinguish between "surface structures" and "deep structures" in the reading of a text. Beneath the surface structure, a text reflects deep structures of conviction and world-ordering. These deep structures are understood as being encoded so that the exegete must understand that the language of a text is functioning as a code. It should be read and analyzed not with a view to determining the referent in any given case, but with a view to determining the "deep structures" from which it ultimately stems and to which it points. Surface structure refers to those contours of a text or piece of writing we can visibly trace, such as the outline of an argument or the flow of a story. Deep structures, by contrast, are those underlying, ordering principles and features that come to concrete expression in the text, but are not actually stated in the text. To return to our earlier example, we may use good principles of grammar as we speak without ever being conscious of the rules of syntax by which we are arranging our words. Or we may choose not to wear a bathrobe to work without ever thinking consciously of the underlying "social syntax" we are following. And yet the underlying principles of grammar and syntax that govern what we say and wear can be deduced from our actual use of language and our customs of dress.

Third, one of the fundamental structuralist principles used to interpret all empirical forms of social behavior and their deep structures is the principle of binary opposition. In analyzing texts, structuralist critics work with categories of opposites, especially those they have observed in a wide variety of texts. Certain pairs of opposites are considered fundamental to all human experience and may be at work in producing any given text. This would include such binary opposites as light/darkness, good/evil, reconciliation/alienation, divine/human, male/female, and others.

The principle of binary opposition applies not only to deep structures but to structuralist method generally. Thus, even in analyzing the surface structures of a text, we can be especially alert to pairs of opposites in the arrangement of the text.

Now that we have considered some of the general perspectives and principles of structuralist criticism, we can examine some examples of how it has been applied to biblical texts.

A classical example of structuralist exegesis as applied to the Old Testament has to do with the creation story in Genesis 1—2. Instead of analyzing the opening chapters of Genesis in terms of classical source criticism and the theory of two creation accounts (1:1—2:4a [P] and 2:4b–25 [J]) with their respective theologies, one structuralist approach concludes that Genesis 1:1—2:1 should be the basic unit in interpretation. This analysis is based on the following structuralist observations: (1) The unit is naturally defined this way since it begins with a reference to God's creating the heavens and earth (1:1) and concludes by noting that the "heavens and the earth were finished" (2:1). (2) The phrase "and God said" occurs ten times (verses 3, 6, 9, 11, 14, 20, 24, 26, 28, and 29). (3) The unit divides into two roughly equal parts with five uses of the expression "and God said" in each: 1:1–19 (containing 207 Hebrew words) and 1:20—2:1 (containing 206 words). The first part describes the creation of the world's inanimate order; the second part describes the creation of the world's living beings. (4) Each half moves toward a similar climax: the first part concluding with a reference to the sun, moon, and stars to rule over the heavens, the second part with humanity to rule over the earth.

Here we see illustrated some of the principles of structuralist exegesis. First, the structures of the text reflect the subject matter and theology of the material. Second, the principle of binary opposition is evident throughout: two roughly equal literary units, inanimate orders/animate orders, rule of luminaries over the inanimate world/rule of humans over the animate world. Third, the focus is on how one reads a text instead of how the author writes a text. How the reader perceives meaning in the text is more important than what the author originally intended.

This structuralist interpretation of Genesis 1:1—2:1 tends to remain at the surface level of the text. Texts may be analyzed to reveal deeper structures, namely, universal patterns of values and convictions. On the basis of folklore studies, a narrative grid has been developed for use in interpreting narrative structures. The grid may be used to determine the structural relationships that appear in narratives (how many appear in any single narrative depends on the story's complexity). Based on this grid, the following chart diagrams the typical roles (called actants by structuralists) present in the narrative structures of most stories, although not all roles are reflected in every story:

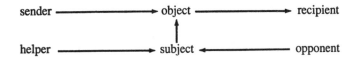

The sender is the originator of an action meant to communicate or transmit some object the recipient needs, to ensure the latter's well-being. The subject is the one sent by the sender to transmit the object to the recipient. The opponent attempts to frustrate the action while the helper assists the subject in carrying out the action.

An analysis of the narrative structure of the Parable of the Good Samaritan (Luke 10:30–35), for example, shows the following actants in the narrative:

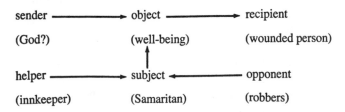

In most narratives (and one can experiment with typical modern plots such as the American Western or TV situation shows), the characters and plots possess a remarkable consistency. In most narratives, life's normalcy or equilibrium is disturbed in some fashion and anarchy or trouble develops. Some subject is sent or takes action to restore order/ well-being, is opposed by the creator of the anarchy or other opponents, and is assisted by a helper or helpers.

The Parable of the Prodigal Son consists of two parts, the first focusing on the prodigal son, the second on the elder brother. Interpreters have often wondered about the relationship between these two parts, even speculating that the story originally ended with the return of the prodigal and that the elder brother episode might have been added later as a way of addressing the Pharisees, or some other group of opponents of early Christianity.

As we have seen previously, structuralist critics eschew approaching the text this way. Their concern is with the story in its present form, the final form of the text. Since it now exists with the elder brother episode, it must be interpreted in that form. In this form, the story may be seen as reflecting a basic folk tale plot, or it may be seen as the story of a character who moves through a sequence of "at home," "away from home," and "at home." Binary oppositions may be seen in various sets of opposites: lostness/foundness, alienation/reconciliation, presence/absence. In fact, one way of structuring the story is to trace the movement from presence (the young man at home) to absence (the young man away from home) to presence (the young man back at home) to absence (the elder brother ironically not "at home" with the father). In this way, the younger brother would typify "presence" or "foundness" while the elder brother would typify "absence" or "lostness." The important point to note is that we are not concerned with how the story functions in the Gospel of Luke, nor with how it reflects the theology of the author of Luke, but rather with how the structures of the story itself function to express meaning in universal categories.

On occasion, plots and characters may startle the reader by their departure from the expected. For example, in the Parable of the Good Samaritan, the Samaritan is the outsider, the heretic, the opposite of what ancient Jewish culture would assume to be the ideal religious person, yet in the story the Samaritan is the subject who brings aid to the recipient (the wounded). In the story of Abraham's sacrifice of Isaac (Gen. 22), God plays two major roles: the deity is the opponent who demands the sacrifice of Isaac and thus produces anarchy and simultaneously the subject who provides the substitute and alleviates the tension. In the narrative of Jacob's wrestling with the angel (God) at the ford of the Jabbok River (Genesis 32:22–32), Jacob is the hero on a quest. In the story, God appears not only as the originator of the quest but also as Jacob's opponent. In the overall structure of the Christ story, God is not only the sender and, in the son, the subject who brings salvation to the world, but also the world's opponent since humankind has to be reconciled to God.

A structuralist interpretation of the book of Psalms has shown that the psalms can be understood in terms of their deep structures. Practically all the statements in the psalms cluster around four actants. These are: A = the protagonist/the psalmist/the just/the community/the king; B = the opposition/the enemy/enemies/the wicked/the nations; C = God; and D = others/witnesses/the faithful/the just/the nations. In individual psalms these four elements assume various roles, generally with A as the recipient, B as the opponent, C as the helper and sender (although sometimes the opponent), and D as the co-recipient. Various binary oppositions run throughout the psalms in the description of persons, states of being, and expectations: life/death, joy/sorrow, lament/praise, weeping/dancing, blessing/curse, and so on. Using such structuralist insights, particular psalms may be analyzed without recourse to actual life situations, biographical consideration, or historical contexts. Paradoxically, references to disorder/evil/sin/anarchy in the psalms and thus to the disruption of normal equilibrium, along with petitions for resolution and redemption give the psalms a strong biographical/narrative flavor. It is our ability to understand and identify, even subconsciously, with these universal structural components in the psalms which has given them their widespread and enduring appeal.

Some biblical narratives lend themselves to even greater abstraction and generalization reflective of mythical structures and symbolism. Mythical structures are found at an even deeper level of abstraction from the text than narrative structures. We noted above how structuralists analyze the narrative structure of the Parable of the Good Samaritan. At a deeper structure or deeper level of abstraction, the parable reflects mythical or paradigmatic structures. The story can be seen as reflecting polar opposites: life/order/health/kingdom of God—death/disorder/woundedness/kingdom of Satan. At the surface level, the Samaritan as a religious outcast would have fit into the camp of the disordered, and the Levite and priest in the arena of the ordered; but well-being in the story is produced by the Samaritan. The reader is thus challenged to venture outside the established order and the ordinary religious boundaries and become, like the Samaritan, a "truly religious person." Thus in the story Jesus challenges the normal mythical pattern by making the antihero into the hero. (One should note the parallels between such structuralist interpretations and medieval allegorical readings: see pp. 20–21.)

The examples we have cited are brief and of only limited value in illustrating the various principles of structuralist criticism. Rather than serving as detailed examples of structuralist exegesis, they are intended to illustrate the general approach. In experimenting with structural exegesis, we need to resist asking historical questions such as who, when, where, and how and instead look for general structures in the text, for examples of binary opposition, and for deep structures reflective of universal interests and concerns.

BIBLIOGRAPHY

General

Barthes, R., *Writing Degree Zero and Elements of Semiology* (London/Boston: Jonathan Cape/Beacon Press, 1967/1970).
Calloud, J., *Structural Analysis of Narrative* (Philadelphia/Missoula: Fortress Press/Scholars Press, 1976).
Calloud, J., "A Few Comments on Structural Semiotics: A Brief Explanation of a Method and Some Explanation of Procedures " in *Semeia* 15 (1979) 51–83.
Culler, J. D., *Structural Poetics: Structuralism, Linguistics and the Story of Literature* (Ithaca, NY/London: Cornell University Press/Routledge & Kegan Paul, 1975), especially pp. 2–54.
Culler, J. D., *The Pursuit of Signs: Semiotics, Literature, Deconstruction* (London/Henley: Routledge & Kegan Paul, 1981).
DeGeorge, R. T. and F. M. DeGeorge (eds.), *The Structuralists: From Marx to Lévi-Strauss* (Garden City/London: Doubleday & Co., 1972).
Detweiler, R., *Story, Sign, and Self: Phenomenology and Structuralism as Literary Critical Methods* (Philadelphia/Missoula: Fortress Press/Scholars Press, 1978).
Greimas, A. J., *Semiotics and Language* (Bloomington: Indiana University Press, 1982).
Kermode, F., *The Genesis of Secrecy: On the Interpretation of Narrative* (Cambridge/London: Harvard University Press, 1979).
Kovacs, B., "Philosophical Foundations for Structuralism " in *Semeia* 10 (1978) 85–105.
*Lane, M. (ed.), *Introduction to Structuralism/Structuralism: A Reader* (New York/London: Basic Books/Jonathan Cape, 1970).
Leach, E. R., *Claude Lévi-Strauss* (rev. ed.; New York/London: Viking Press/Fontana Press, 1974).
*Propp, V., *Morphology of the Folktale* (Austin: University of Texas Press, 1968; first published 1928).
Ricoeur, P., *The Conflict of Interpretations: Essays in Hermeneutics* (Evanston: Northwestern University Press, 1974), especially pp. 27–96.

Ricoeur, P., *Essays on Biblical Interpretation/On Biblical Interpretation* (Philadelphia/London: Fortress Press/SPCK, 1980/1981).

*Robey, D. (ed.), *Structuralism: An Introduction* (London/New York: Oxford University Press, 1973).

Scholes, R., *Structuralism in Literature: An Introduction* (New Haven/London: Yale University Press, 1974).

Biblical Structuralism

Barthes, R. et al., *Structural Analysis and Biblical Exegesis: Interpretational Essays* (Pittsburgh/Edinburgh: Pickwick Press/T. & T. Clark, 1974).

*Barton, J., *Reading the Old Testament: Method in Biblical Study* (London/Philadelphia: Darton, Longman and Todd/Westminster Press, 1984) 104–39.

Bovon, F. et al., *Structural Analysis and Biblical Exegesis: Interpretational Essays* (Pittsburgh: Pickwick Press, 1974).

Doty, W., "Linguistics and Biblical Criticism" in *Journal of the American Academy of Religion* 41 (1973) 114–21.

Greenwood, D. C., *Structuralism and the Biblical Text* (New York: Mouton de Gruyter, 1985).

Jacobson, R., "The Structuralists and the Bible " in *Interpretation* 28(1974)146–64.

*Keegan, T. J., *Interpreting the Bible: A Popular Introduction to Biblical Hermeneutics* (Mahwah: Paulist Press, 1985) 40–72.

Patte, D., *What Is Structural Exegesis?* (Philadephia/London: Fortress Press/ SCM Press, 1976).

Polzin, R. M., *Biblical Structuralism: Method and Subjectivity in the Study of Ancient Texts* (Philadelphia/Missoula: Fortress Press/Scholars Press, 1977).

Robbins, V. K., "Structuralism in Biblical Interpretation and Theology " *The Thomist* 42 (1978) 349–72.

*Rogerson, J. W., "Recent Literary Structuralist Approaches to Biblical Interpretation" in *The Churchman* 90 (1976) 165–77.

Tollers, V. L. and J. R. Maier, *The Bible in Its Literary Milieu* (Grand Rapids: Eerdmans Publishing Company, 1979).

Old Testament

Alonso-Schökel, L., "The Poetic Structure of Psalms 42–44 " in *Journal for the Study of the Old Testament* 1 (1976) 4–11; 3 (1977) 61–65.

Bar-Efrat, S., "Some Observations on the Analysis of Structure in Biblical Narrative " in *Vetus Testamentum* 30 (1980) 154–73.

Buss, M. (ed.), *Encounter with the Text: Form and History in the Hebrew Bible* (Missoula/Philadelphia: Scholars Press/Fortress Press, 1979).

*Collins, T., "Decoding the Psalms: A Structural Approach to the Psalter " in *Journal for the Study of the Old Testament* 37 (1987) 41–60.

Culley, R. C. (ed.), *Classical Hebrew Narrative (Semeia* 3; Missoula: Scholars Press, 1975).

Culley, R. C. (ed.), *Perspectives on Old Testament Narrative (Semeia* 15; Missoula: Scholars Press, 1979).

Fokkelman, J. P., *Narrative Art in Genesis: Specimens of Stylistic and Structural Analysis* (Assen: Van Gorcum, 1975).

Fokkelman, J. P., *Narrative Art and Poetry in the Books of Samuel: A Full Inter-pretation Based on Stylistic and Structural Analyses* (4 vols.; Assen: Van Gorcum, 1980–).

Jobling, D., *The Sense of Biblical Narrative: Three Structural Analyses in the Old Testament* (Sheffield: JSOT Press, 1978).

Leach, E. R., *Genesis as Myth and Other Essays* (London: Jonathan Cape, 1969).

Leach, E. R. and D. A. Aycock, *Structuralist Interpretations of Biblical Myth* (Cambridge/New York: Cambridge University Press, 1983).

Patte, D. (ed.), *Genesis 2 and 3: Kaleidoscopic Structural Readings (Semeia* 18; Chico: Scholars Press, 1980).

Roth, W., "Structural Interpretations of 'Jacob at the Jabbok' (Genesis 32:22–32) " in *Biblical Research* 22 (1977) 51–62.

New Testament

Calloud, J., "Toward a Structural Analysis of the Gospel of Mark" in *Semeia* 16 (1980) 133–65.

Crespy, G., "The Parable of the Good Samaritan: An Essay in Structural Research " in *Semeia* 2 (1974) 27–50.

*Crossan, J. D., "Structural Analysis and the Parables of Jesus " in *Linguistica Biblica* 29/30 (1973) 41–51.

Kodjak, A., *A Structural Analysis of the Sermon on the Mount* (New York: Mouton de Gruyter, 1987).

Patte, D. (ed.), *Semiology and Parables: An Exploration of the Possibilities Offered by Structuralism for Exegesis* (Pittsburgh: Pickwick Press, 1975).

Patte, D. and A. Patte, *Structural Exegesis: From Theory to Practice. Exegesis of Mark 15 and 16. Hermeneutical Implications* (Philadelphia: Fortress Press, 1978).

Patte, D., *Paul's Faith and the Power of the Gospel: A Structural Introduction to the Pauline Letters* (Philadelphia: Fortress Press, 1983).

Via, D., *Kerygma and Comedy in the New Testament: A Structuralist Approach to Hermeneutic* (Philadelphia: Fortress Press, 1975).

Via, D., "Parable and Example Story: A Literary-Structuralist Approach " in *Linguistica Biblica* 25/26 (1973) 21–30.

CHAPTER 10

CANONICAL CRITICISM:

The Sacred Text of Synagogue and Church

The Bible is the sacred Scripture of synagogue and church. This means that the writings comprising the Jewish and Christian Scriptures are endowed with a special authority and are granted a special role by these believing communities. Earlier in the book, we noted some factors involved both in treating a text as sacred and in the interaction between sacred texts and religious communities (see pp. 13–14, 17–18). At this point we need to note some of these issues in more detail.

The sacred texts—the canon—of a religious community are what may be called foundational documents in that they are constitutive and regulatory for the life and faith of the community. This status of canonical texts is based on the belief that they reflect and bear testimony to truth in a unique and unrepeatable manner. The belief about the texts' relationship to truth is usually undergirded by claims about their origination through special inspiration and about their character as revelatory documents. As foundational texts, they are understood as embodying and reflecting, in at least embryonic fashion, the essence of the faith and practice of the community.

This privileged status ascribed to canonical texts means that they are read and understood in the believing communities in a manner different from all other texts. The believing communities function as interpretative communities that read the Scriptures using given conventions and strategies. First, the text is read with expectations that differ from those brought to any other text. The believing community reads and listens to the Bible assuming its relevance and expecting to hear through its words a witness to, if not the voice of, God. Through the Scriptures, believers anticipate an existential encounter with truth. Second, the universe of the sacred text, or to use structuralist terminology, the semantic universe of the text, challenges the reader and hearer to share its world and convictions. A canonical text thus confronts the audience with an autocratic claim to faith acceptance; it authoritatively imposes itself. Third, canonical texts are read with a degree of receptivity rarely extended to other texts. When the believer and believing community read the Scriptures, they do so as "believers." This means they already accept the faith presented and presumed by the text and thus hear the sacred text in light of the prior faith. The text is thus approached with a "preunderstanding." The text is heard within the context of the faith. A secondary consequence of this preunderstanding and contextual hearing is the tendency to ignore or indulge differences, inconsistencies, and problems within the text. The reader fills out and smooths over differences and difficulties within the text in light of the overall cohesion of the canon and in terms of the community's faith perspective.

In recent years, there has been a vigorous call to read and exegete biblical texts explicitly as canonical Scripture. Different terminology has been used to designate this type of exegesis: canonical/canon criticism, canonical hermeneutics, canonical exegesis, canonical interpretation, and so forth. Several considerations related to canonical interpretation should be noted.

(1) The canonical approach is synchronic and thus text-reader oriented. In this regard, canonical reading of texts has many parallels to redaction criticism and structuralist interpretations. The text to be exegeted is the final form, namely, the form of the text that achieved canonical status. The reader is understood specifically as a reader standing within the believing community for whom the text is canonical. This means that the interpreter is not concerned with the issues characteristic of historical-critical approaches—the earliest or pre-canonical form of the text or tradition, the original intention of the writer, events and experiences behind the text, or the historical/sociological/psychological context that gave birth to the text. These may be given some consideration but are not the decisive factors for reading and understanding the text. (Already in his *Confessions*, Augustine wrestled with the issue of the "truth of things" vs. the "intention of the speaker [Moses]," preferring the former since it was difficult to know whether "Moses meant this [interpretation] and wished this to be understood from his account" [Book 12. Chapters 23—24]. Thus the tension between a canonical reading and the original author's intent was already an issue for Augustine.)

(2) A canonical reading of a text will vary depending upon which believing community is doing the reading and which canon is being read. Jewish, Catholic, Orthodox, and Protestant scriptural canons dif-

fer considerably from one another. Simultaneously, the faith perspective within which canonical texts are read also varies considerably, not only among the major religious groups themselves, but also among various denominations within the same religious tradition. Even the content of books such as Esther and Daniel differs from one canon to another. Obviously, Christians read the Old Testament with different expectations and different theological preunderstanding than Jewish readers. In other words, the symbolic worlds and the reading conventions of Jews and Christians differ appreciably.

Even the canonical ordering of the books in the Jewish Bible and the Christian Old Testament illustrates a major difference in approach and preunderstanding. The books in the Jewish Bible are ordered into three divisions—Torah, Prophets, and Writings. Priority is given to the Torah. The medieval Jewish philosopher Maimonides (1135–1204) describes these divisions as three concentric circles with the Torah in the center and the other two divisions as illustrative commentary arranged in descending order of authority. This structure and its underlying assumptions indicate that the books in the second and third divisions are to be read looking backward—the Prophets and the Writings are read in the shadow of the Torah. The Christian canon, on the other hand, is structured into the four following divisions—Torah, History, Poetry, and Prophets. Placing the prophets with their predictions last encouraged the Christian to look beyond the Old Testament and to read the preceding material with a forward-looking rather than a backward-looking orientation.

(3) Canonization separated the meaning of the texts from dependence on their historical or original use. Texts that once grew out of and were rooted in particular historical contexts and communities have been detached from such contexts and made accessible to a wider and universal audience. In canonizing the literature, the believing communities declared the writings to be universally and permanently relevant and accessible. The canonical process loosened the texts from specific historical settings and transcended the original addresses. Synagogue and church declared that the historically conditioned and original meaning of the Scriptures was not their only nor their most important meaning. Prophetic preaching, for example, was originally addressed to specific historical and rhetorical situations; because the situation was known, explanatory details were not required. When such material became part of a later literary document and the memory of the rhetorical situation had faded, then the content of such speeches assumed a more genera-

lized cast. Isaiah's speeches in 1:2–20 and 2:6–22, for example, were probably originally delivered in light of the recent devastating earthquake under Uzziah (Amos 1:2; Zech. 14:5). The material itself, however, provides no clues that unequivocally point to, and none that demand, such a setting. Thus these two speeches, now severed from their original setting, lend themselves to interpretation in general and/or futuristic categories. It was not just the canonical process per se that dehistoricized and generalized the material; the nature and content of the speeches and the editorial process had early on already given such material this open-ended, unhistorically conditioned quality. Now in their canonical form, the reader encounters the material without specific historical associations.

An example of the deinstitutionalization with the resultant generalization of material can be seen in the case of the psalms. Most if not all of the psalms were originally composed for and utilized in services of worship. The editorial and canonical process which shaped the Psalter produced a book of compositions whose original association with Israel's worship is almost totally obscured.

(4) A canonical approach avoids the atomization and thus the isolated interpretation of texts. A text is to be read as part of the Bible in its entirety, not as an independent, single unit. Each passage is read as part of a biblical book, and the biblical book is seen as part of an even larger entity—the canon as a whole. The whole is thus greater and more authoritative than any of its parts. Thus even a biblical book has only penultimate authority since it is the Bible as a whole that possesses final canonical authority. (It can be argued that even the canon has only relative authority since the Bible is read in the context of a believing, interpretive community whose faith and beliefs provide the lens for interpreting the Scriptures. The faith of the community places contraints on the possible meanings just as the faith of the community established the limits of the canon initially.) The believing community reads and hears the Scriptures, assuming the canon's internal cohesion. Thus, even a passage from the Old Testament read in the church will be heard in light of the New Testament. Texts are read and heard in interaction and concert. The mutual interplay among texts, which results produced an accumulative effort, transcends any one text. This does not mean that the believing community should or does suppress the plurality and fluidity in the biblical writings. (The church, for example, consistently opposed any move to reduce the number of the Gospels or to replace the four with a single harmonization.) The assumption is, however, that the

understanding and interpretation of an individual text must conform to the constraints resulting from the text's existence as part of a larger work.

(5) Canonical criticism is overtly theological in its approach. In terms of our diagrams on pages 24–25, a canonical approach interprets the Bible as a mimetic reflection of reality, as a vehicle for understanding the will of God. The Bible is Scripture and must be so interpreted. If historical-critical studies ask what the individual units and books in the Bible originally meant, canonical criticism is concerned with the meaning of the text for the canonizing community and with the present meaning of the text.

Some examples can illustrate the character and method of a canonical reading and interpretation of biblical texts. The book of Isaiah provides one of the clearest illustrations of the impact of canonical reading. Historical criticism has demonstrated with a reasonable degree of certainty that large portions of Isaiah, at least chapters 40—55, come from the sixth century. Second Isaiah, as this material is designated, has been attached to and become a part of a collection attributed to Isaiah who functioned during the eighth-century reigns of Kings Uzziah, Jotham, Ahaz, and Hezekiah (see Isa. 1:1). (Third Isaiah, chapters 56—66, about which there is less certainty, has undergone a similar fate.) Thus, in the editorial process leading to the book's canonical shape and content, chapters 40—55 were loosed from any explicit association with the events of the sixth century. (References to Cyrus, as in Isa. 45:1, do not absolutely demand reading chapters 40—55 with reference to the sixth century.) Simultaneously, they were "rehistoricized" and associated with the prophet Isaiah and the eighth century. This shift had the effect of intensifying the futuristic cast of the material and the redemptive character of its content. Likewise it strengthened an understanding of Isaiah and his prophetic preaching in terms of the prediction of future events:

> By the spirit of might he [Isaiah] saw the last things,
>   and comforted those who mourned in Zion.
> He revealed what was to occur to the end of time,
>   and the hidden things before they came to pass.
>
> (Sirach 48:24–25)

As we noted earlier in this chapter (see section 3), in the editorial process, historically specific oracles of Isaiah assumed a generalized tone. Isaiah 9:2–7 and 11:1–9 once spoke about a particular contemporary ruler on the throne of David (in this case probably King Ahaz). In their more dehistoricized general form, such passages lent themselves to and, in fact, practically required an idealistic and messianic interpretation. In their edited canonical form, the prophet did not appear to be speaking while looking around at his contemporaries; he appeared to be looking forward to one who would come. As part of a Christian canon these Isaianic texts defy a reading which does not simultaneously resonate in some fashion with the early church's claims about Jesus.

A canonical exegesis must take into consideration not only the final form of the text but also the final form of the text as part of canonical Scripture. There are no First, Second, and Third Isaiahs in Scripture, only the book of Isaiah. Certainly the Christian community could hardly think of Yahweh's chosen leader in Isaiah, solely in terms of Isaiah 9:2–7 and 11:1–9, and without regard for such texts as Isaiah 52:13—53:12. Historical-critical considerations might argue that the two sets of texts derive from different contexts and originally referred to different figures (although this might be questioned even on historical-critical grounds). Their presence now within one book encourages association in interpretation.

A text from the book of Ecclesiastes could be treated differently depending on whether one is working from historical-critical or canonical perspectives. A strong and reasonable case can be built for Ecclesiastes 12:13–14 being a late editorial addition to the book. Throughout much of the remainder of the book a rather skeptical and pessimistic view is taken of life and religion. Historical critics assume that the original book was completely skeptical in outlook. The later addition, however, suggests to the reader that one should not give in to doubt and unbelief, that is, it relativizes the preceding skeptical advice. The final form of the canonical text has overridden the skepticism of an earlier form. Obviously a canonical reading must take 12:13–14 into consideration in exegeting other texts in the book. The pessimistic thrust of the book is thus mitigated by the optimistic conclusion.

The content of one book may also relativize the content of another. Throughout the book of Ecclesiastes, no hope is held out for believing in immortality or the resurrection of the dead. In fact Ecclesiastes 3:19 declares that humans suffer the same fate as animals; both die without hope. If this text is interpreted within a canon that contains the Wisdom of Solomon (as in Orthodox and Catholic circles), then the assertion of the Ecclesiastes text is highly relativized, since Wisdom 3:1–9 clearly affirms immortality and rewards after death. When Ecclesiastes 3:19 is read as part of a canon containing the New Testament with its strong and pervasive emphasis on the resurrection, the content of the Ecclesiastes text is even further relativized.

So far, we have illustrated canonical criticism primarily with reference to the Old Testament. The approach has similar implications for New Testament interpretation. Canonical interpretation emphasizes that the New Testament should be interpreted in terms of its final canonical form. Several general inferences drawn from such a conclusion differ radically from typical historical-critical perspectives.

(1) Reconstructed settings in the life of Jesus should not be given priority in interpreting the sayings or teachings of Jesus. Much modern interpretation of the teachings of Jesus relies on the assumption that these teachings must be freed from their present literary contexts and projected back into the socio-politico-religious circumstances of the historical Jesus in order to be understood properly. A canonical interpretation would conclude that such hypothetical reconstructions are of benefit only if they contribute to an understanding of the present form and construal of the text.

(2) Pre-canonical literary compositions may not be appealed to as the key for understanding canonical compositions. For example, the reconstructed document "Q," which was apparently used by the authors of Matthew and Luke, may aid in understanding how traditions and sayings were once formulated and transmitted but cannot be assigned any determinative authoritative status in interpreting the final canonical form of the biblical materials. Similarly, although the Gospel of Luke and the book of Acts were apparently originally a single composition, they were canonized as two separate works and in the final analysis must be so interpreted.

(3) The chronological order in which biblical books originated is not decisive for exegesis. Modern scholarship tends to assume, for example, that 1 Thessalonians was the first written of Paul's epistles. In the canon, however, Romans opens the collection of Pauline writings. In establishing this order, the early church predisposed the reader to interpret the remainder of Paul's writings in light of the book of Romans. The canonical construal of the material thus severed the letters of Paul from their chronological moorings. A canonical reading thus differs from one based on chronological considerations.

In carrying out a canonical interpretation of a passage, the interpreter focuses not on the original authorial intention or the circumstances of the original situation but on how the text in its present form and construal bears the theological witness to faith and the gospel.

BIBLIOGRAPHY

The Development of the Biblical Canons

Aland, K., *The Problem of the New Testament Canon* (Oxford/Westminster, MD: A. R. Mowbray & Co./Canterbury Press, 1962).

Attridge, H. W. (ed.), *The Formation of the New Testament Canon* (New York: Paulist Press, 1983).

Barton, J., *Oracles of God: Perceptions of Ancient Prophecy in Israel after the Exile* (London: Darton, Longman and Todd, 1986).

Beckwith, R., *The Old Testament Canon of the New Testament Church and Its Background in Early Judaism* (London/Grand Rapids: SPCK/Eerdmans Publishing Company, 1985).

Best, E., "Scripture, Tradition and the Canon of the New Testament " in *Bulletin of the John Rylands University Library of Manchester* 61 (1979) 259–89.

Bruns, G. L., "Canon and Power in the Hebrew Sciptures " in *Critical Inquiry* 10 (1984) 462–80.

*von Campenhausen, H., *The Formation of the Christian Bible* (Philadelphia: Fortress Press, 1972).

Detweiler, R., "What is a Sacred Text?" in *Semeia* 31 (1985) 213–30.

Dunn, J. D. G., "Levels of Canonical Authority" in *Horizons in Biblical Theology* 4 (1982) 13–60.

Farmer, W. R. and D. M. Farkasfalvy, *The Formation of the New Testament Canon: An Ecumenical Approach* (New York: Paulist Press, 1983).

Gamble, H. Y., *The New Testament Canon: Its Making and Meaning* (Philadelphia: Fortress Press, 1985).

Leiman, S. Z. (ed.), *The Canon and Masorah of the Hebrew Bible: An Introductory Reader* (New York: KTAV, 1974).

Leiman, S. Z., *The Canonization of Hebrew Scripture: The Talmudic and Midrashic Evidence* (Hamden, CT: Archon Books, 1976).

Lewis, J. P., "What Do We Mean by Jabneh?" in *Journal of Bible and Religion* 32 (1964) 125–32.

Lightstone, J. N., "The Formation of the Biblical Canon in Judaism of Late Antiquity: Prolegomena to a General Reassessment " in *Studies in Religion* 8 (1979) 135–42.

McDonald, L. M., *The Formation of the Christian Biblical Canon* (Nashville: Abingdon Press, 1988).

*Sundberg, A. C., Jr., *The Old Testament of the Early Church* (Cambridge/London: Harvard University Press, 1964).

Sundberg, A. C., Jr., "The Protestant Old Testament Canon: Should It be Reexamined?" in *Catholic Biblical Quarterly* 28 (1966) 194–203.

Sundberg, A. C., Jr., "The 'Old Testament': A Christian Canon " in *Catholic Biblical Quarterly* 30 (1968) 143–55.

Canonical Criticism

Ackroyd, P. A., "Original Text and Canonical Text " in *Union Seminary Quarterly Review* 32 (1977) 166–73.

*Barr, J., *Holy Scripture: Canon, Authority, Criticism* (London/Philadelphia: Oxford University Press/Westminster Press, 1983).

*Barton, J., *Reading the Old Testament: Method in Biblical Study* (London/Philadelphia: Darton, Longman and Todd/Westminster Press, 1984) 77–103, 140–57.

Brown, R. E., *The Critical Meaning of the Bible* (New York: Paulist Press, 1981).

Brueggemann, W., *The Creative Word: Canon as a Model for Biblical Education* (Philadelphia: Fortress Press, 1982).

Childs, B. S., "The Old Testament as Scripture of the Church " in *Concordia Theological Monthly* 43 (1972) 709–22.

Childs, B. S., "The Exegetical Significance of Canon for the Study of the Old Testament " in *Supplements to Vetus Testamentum* (vol. 29; Leiden: E. J. Brill, 1978) 66–80.

*Childs, B. S., *Introduction to the Old Testament as Scripture* (London/Philadelphia: SCM Press/Fortress Press, 1979).

*Childs, B. S., *The New Testament as Canon: An Introduction* (London/Philadelphia: SCM Press/Fortress Press, 1985).

Coats, G. W. and B. O. Long (eds.), *Canon and Authority: Essays In Old Testament Religion and Theology* (Philadelphia; Fortress Press, 1977).

Fowl, S., "The Canonical Approach of Brevard Childs " in *Expository Times* 96 (1985) 173–75.

Keegan, T. J., *Interpreting the Bible: A Popular Introduction to Biblical Hermeneutics* (Mahwah, NJ: Paulist Press, 1985) 131–64.

Lemcio, E., "The Gospels and Canonical Criticism " in *Biblical Theology Bulletin* 11 (1981) 114–22.

Roth, W., *Isaiah* (Knox Preaching Guides; Atlanta: John Knox Press, 1987).

Sanders, J. A., *Torah and Canon* (Philadelphia: Fortress Press, 1974).

Sanders, J. A., *Canon and Community: A Guide to Canonical Criticism* (Philadelphia: Fortress Press, 1984).

*Sanders, J. A., *From Sacred Story to Sacred Text* (Philadelphia: Fortress Press, 1987).

Sheppard, G. T., "Canonization: Hearing the Voice of the Same God Through Historically Dissimilar Traditions " in *Interpretation* 37 (1982) 21–33.

Siker, J., "The Theology of the Sabbath in the Old Testament: A Canonical Approach " in *Studia Biblica et Theologica* 11 (1981) 5–20.

Spina, F. A., "Canonical Criticism: Childs Versus Sanders " in *Interpreting God's Word for Today: An Inquiry into Hermeneutics from a Biblical Theological Perspective* (ed. W. McCown and J. E. Massey; Anderson, IN: Warner Press, 1982) 165–94.

Steinmetz, D. C., "The Superiority of Pre-Critical Exegesis " in *Theology Today* 37 (1980) 27–38.

Stuhlmacher, P., *Historical Criticism and Theological Interpretation of Scripture* (Philadephia: Fortress Press, 1977).

CHAPTER 11

Integrating EXEGETICAL PROCEDURES

The goal of exegesis is an informed understanding of a text. All the exegetical procedures and types of criticism which we have discussed in the preceding chapters have this as their aim.

At this point, the student may feel a bit overwhelmed by the diversity of critical aproaches which can be utilized in exegeting a biblical text and somewhat submerged in a mass of what appear to be prescriptive directions. Here one may wish to ask, "Is all of this necessary merely to understand a text?" "How is it possible to use and integrate all of these procedures?" Before discussing some of the more practical aspects of exegesis, several suggestions perhaps should be made at this juncture.

(1) The task of biblical exegesis is not unrelated to much of the work that is done in general theological education. In fact, many courses which involve the reading and analysis of sources, whether primary or secondary, present occasions for doing forms of exegesis. Whenever one encounters a text and asks such questions as, "How should I read this text?" "What does this mean?" "Why is this said this way?" "Why does the text say this and not something else?" "How can I rethink what is said so as to give it expression in my own words?" one is engaged in exegesis. Thus exegesis, even of technical works, is not an activity strange to theological students. We should recognize much of our work as exegetical in orientation and be conscious that much that is learned from the interrogation of a text in a non-biblical area has relevance for and can be carried over to the interrogation of a biblical text.

(2) Practically all biblical studies, even if they are not designated as "exegetical," are relevant to the task of exegesis. Introductory and other courses on the Bible explore facets of the nature and content of biblical documents, the history and religion of Israel and the early church, and the culture and background of biblical texts. Many of these topics

already contribute to an understanding of many of the procedures of exegesis as well as provide data and insights needed in exegetical work. Thus general biblical studies either engage in exegesis or provide substance and evidence that can be employed in exegesis.

(3) Not all the exegetical procedures we have discussed are relevant to every text. Frequently, for example, no significant textual problems will be encountered. Although there are thousands of variations among the Greek texts of the New Testament, most of these textual variants are not of any great consequence for interpreting a passage. With practically all texts, some forms of criticism will be of more significance than others but seldom will all be of crucial importance.

(4) Exegetical procedures are frequently carried out and critical methods utilized although the exegete may not be consciously aware of doing "grammatical analysis" or some other such activity. Most exegetical methods are based on the operation of common sense, intuition, and good judgment. Whenever a text is studied with these factors in operation, many of the technical forms of criticism are already being utilized. Although the terminology used for such criticisms and the conscious formulation of such methods are of rather recent vintage, good exegetes throughout the centuries have been concerned with the issues which the methodologies articulate. The same condition can certainly be equally characteristic of the contemporary situation.

In "doing exegesis," the student should realize that, as we suggested earlier, the various exegetical procedures are not related to one another in any strict architectonic fashion. That is, no mechanical system of steps or stages in the exegetical process can be set up and rigidly followed. One cannot, let us say, first do the textual-critical analysis, and then proceed to a second step and so on. Frequently, the interests and issues of the various criticisms are interrelated. Textual-critical conclusions, for example, may depend upon what conclusions have been reached from form-critical considerations. A particular textual variant may appear more original than another because it fits better the form of the material. Textual-critical conclusions could certainly be influenced by grammatical analysis.

An appropriate way of proceeding in doing an exegesis of a passage is to let the questions and issues arise from the text itself. This is often best achieved by reading and rereading the passage in its context several times. As the exegete rereads the passage, questions of various kinds will naturally present themselves to the reader. If the same questions or the same types of questions keep surfacing as the exegete rereads the passage, they should be listed and classified into appropriate categories. If, for example, certain words or phrases continue to remain obscure, and they do not "fall into place" in subsequent readings, they provide part of the exegete's agenda and may involve some word study. Or, if all the words and phrases themselves are clear, but they still continue to puzzle the reader, one may discover that the syntax of the sentence or paragraph needs to be untangled, and this will provide a different sort of agenda and move into grammatical analysis. It may be that on a first or second reading of the passage, the exegete notices a significant variation of wording referred to in a footnote, so significant that it might substantially alter one's final interpretation of the passage. In this case, the textual-critical problem sets the agenda.

To put it another way, the text itself should set the interpretive agenda whenever possible. This in no way suggests that the interpreter can bring to the text a mind which is a "blank tablet" for this is clearly impossible. In fact, every time we read a text, we bring to the text the total accumulation of who we are—our previous history, our previously accumulated knowledge, our outlook, our individual concerns, and our preunderstanding of what the text or passage means. It has been said that a literary work is like a picnic—the author brings the words and the reader brings the meaning. Although clearly an exaggeration, the saying nonetheless is partially true. Rather than denying that each interpreter reads texts with preunderstanding and many presuppositions, we should recognize that this is inherent in any kind of interpretation. Rather than denying it, we should rather recognize it, and capitalize on it. This is best achieved by admitting our presuppositions, trying as best we can to recognize what they are, how we came to hold them, and then allow for them as we interpret a passage. We should not simply read our own interpretation into a passage; that is eisegesis not exegesis. We should rather read a passage through our understanding which we bring to the text. This understanding can be broadened, modified, or deepened as we exegete the text.

Even if we bring our previous understanding to a text as we begin to interpret it, the text still possesses an autonomy which we should respect. The interpreter should allow the text to speak for itself. By this we mean that the text possesses its own voice, and at this stage the interpreter should learn to listen. Far too frequently, the interpreter is too eager to speak to the text, or even into the text, rather than listen attentively to it. When this occurs, the interpreter succeeds in hearing his or her own voice, not the voice of the text. By granting some autonomy to the text, and allowing it to speak its own message, the interpreter will discover that the text can not only set its own agenda, but a full one at that. As questions begin to surface, the exegete's task begins to take shape. The exegete's art consists in the ability to appreciate the nature and genre of the text at hand and what questions are appropriate to address to that particular type of text and to sort out the genuinely important questions, knowing which exegetical techniques and criticisms are most appropriate for addressing these questions, knowing which tools and books are most suitable for applying these techniques, and knowing how to deploy them efficiently and imaginatively so as to produce an informed and coherent interpretation of a text.

By insisting that the text possesses its own autonomy and by urging the interpreter to listen first and speak later, we do not wish to eliminate the possibility of coming to a text with a previously defined agenda. Quite often as one is engaged in a particular type of research, for example, an investigation in which one is trying to reconstruct the history of a particular period, it will become obvious that a biblical text, or a set of texts, provides the most useful set of sources for doing so. In this case, one may quite legitimately approach the biblical text with previously formulated questions, namely, "What historical information does it provide about the period under consideration?" Or, "How does it illuminate or illustrate the historical period?" The interpreter, thus, may come to a text, knowing in advance that certain kinds of questions and these questions only, will be asked of a text. The interpreter's task in this situation is being able to recognize, first, whether after reading the texts, this is a legitimate question or type of approach and, second, whether other kinds of questions may be asked of the text, perhaps with as much justification, and perhaps to greater benefit.

The beginning exegete, then, should bring all previous understanding to bear on a particular text, define as clearly as possible the kinds of questions one is asking of the text and that the text requires asking, and then determine which techniques and modes of criticism are most appropriate in addressing these questions.

Exegesis, as conceived and described in this volume, occurs when a person reads a biblical text and, based on an informed understanding of this text, develops a first-hand interpretation of the text. Throughout our discussion, it has been assumed that the primary encounter will occur between the reader and the biblical text itself and that all other investigations will be carried out toward this end. Consequently, we have emphasized the use of primary tools, such as dictionaries, concordances, and encyclopedias, and other aids to inform the exegete's own formulation of the questions to be answered and the interpretation to be achieved.

This approach has been followed consciously because beginning exegetes often misconceive the nature and task of exegesis. Exegesis does not consist in consulting various commentaries on a given passage and from these commentaries constructing a single interpretation unifying the various observations and remarks of the commentators. Approaching exegesis in this fashion only produces a mosaic of commentaries, and ultimately means that the interpreter only directly engages the commentaries themselves, while the text is encountered only indirectly, if at all. When this approach is taken to exegesis, it is like an artist who paints a picture by cutting up other artists' pictures and pasting them together. To develop an understanding of a text through the exclusive use of commentaries on the passage can only produce a derivative interpretation because the questions asked by the commentators remain central and primary. Granting such dominance to biblical commentators also produces a kind of exegetical tyranny where the beginning interpreter assumes that the commentators' questions are not only the right questions to be asked of a text, but also the important ones, or even the only ones.

Rather than conceiving exegesis as the process through which the interpreter constructs a sort of collage of commentators' opinions, exegesis should be a more direct engagement between interpreter and text. By stressing the first-hand quality of the interpretive process, we want to underscore the autonomy of the interpreter. It is important for the beginning exegete to realize that the questions of a novice, even if they later turn out to be the wrong or ill-formulated questions, are nevertheless the questions a novice must ask. Only by asking the questions a text truly poses for the beginner will it be possible to develop skill in learning to interrogate a text. The beginning exegete should not be intimidated by the erudition of biblical commentaries and scholars, and in doing so allow them to set the agenda. Much is gained by reading a text for oneself, learning to formulate one's own questions and issues based on a careful reading of the text, and doing so with both independence and imagination.

In calling for this primary level of reading and interpreting the biblical documents, we are not minimizing the work of biblical commentators and the scholarly guild, for they render a valuable service to those who read, study, and interpret texts, both novices and veterans. We merely want to insist upon the primacy of the interpreter's task, and encourage even the beginning exegete to develop both independence and imagination. A better use of commentaries and other books or articles, which spell out the interpretations of particular books or texts, is as a source for secondary consultation and orientation rather than as a primary reference. Commentaries function best to provide a control for the interpreter's own hypotheses and intuitions. They are best viewed as the work of more experienced interpreters whose opinions and views can be consulted rather than taken as unquestionably authoritative. For this reason, for the student who wishes to develop some expertise in doing exegesis, they will always function in a secondary role. (Lists of commentaries on individual books may be found in the standard Old Testament and New Testament introductions and evaluations of individual commentaries and commentary series may be found in the standard biblical bibliographies; see the bibliography to chapter one.)

If exegesis is not merely the compilation of statements and opinions of various commentators, neither is it a report of one's research per se. Beginning exegetes often err in assuming that an exegesis paper consists in reporting or organizing into some systematic fashion all the research one has carried out in analyzing a passage. Some of this is done, to be sure, but exegesis is more than this. Rather than collecting and organizing all the *data* one has uncovered, exegesis consists of a coherent *interpretation* of the passage based upon a careful perusal of the data and an informed, competent reading. This requires an additional step, where one deploys rather than reports this information, arranging it into meaningful sections and patterns of argumentation so that the passage itself is unfolded in an illuminating fashion. Rather than constituting the exegesis, one's research on various facets of the passage provides that from which the exegesis is prepared. One's research informs the interpretation; it does not constitute it.

Quite often, beginning exegetes err by including within an exegesis paper numerous historical, lexicographical, linguistic, and many other types of details, without at the same time deploying them into an overall scheme which succeeds in genuinely illuminating the passage. This passion for details, though commendable in and of itself, should be coupled with a passion for coherence and overall clarity. The exegete must ask, at the end of the exegesis, whether the paper as a whole illuminates or obfuscates a passage. It may be full of factually correct information yet fail to illuminate or display an understanding of the passage in any appreciable fashion.

A third mistake beginning exegetes often make is assuming that the best way of unfolding the analysis is in a verse-by-verse fashion or in a series of word studies. While this is true in some instances, it is not true in every instance. Some biblical passages lend themselves quite readily to such an organizational structure while others do not. The most important consideration in deciding on the structure of an exegesis is whether it is sufficiently comprehensive to do justice to all the important aspects of the passage, yet pliable enough to provide the framework for unfolding an illuminating and coherent interpretation.

Here again, the text itself must offer the best guidance. Some texts, because they unfold an argument in sequential, step-by-step fashion or reflect a particular genre structure, may require an exegetical outline which both exposes and illuminates this structure. Other texts, by contrast, perhaps because they are narrative, are best treated thematically or in some other fashion. The exegesis may be arranged according to major themes which emerge from the passage, and under the treatment of these themes it may be possible for the exegete to treat all the important questions which arise throughout the passage.

It should be remembered that an exegesis is an informed understanding of a passage based on a first-hand engagement with and a thinking through of the text. How one's understanding of the text is actually presented finally becomes a decision of the exegete, and at this point the exegete learns first hand how vitally related form is to content and how both shape meaning. Once the exegete has developed an understanding of content and has articulated the meaning of the passage, the remaining task is to decide upon the appropriate form in which both of these can be conveyed.

Throughout our discussion of the various techniques of exegesis, we have introduced the more practical concerns only incidentally as we have explained the more theoretical nature of each of the types of criticism which might inform an understanding of a passage. At this point, we now turn to the more explicitly practical concerns of preparing an exegesis.

(1) Allow the text to set the agenda. We have already stressed the importance of allowing the questions to arise out of dialogue with the text itself. As the exegete reads a biblical passage, then rereads it several times, preferably in the original but in at least more than one translation, questions and issues of various sorts will begin to emerge. As these become formulated, the exegete will naturally begin to sift them out and arrange them in some order of priority, so that all the crucial ones are addressed.

(2) Let the questions point to the appropriate methodology, exegetical

technique, or type of criticism. At this stage, the exegete will need to possess a general understanding of the various dimensions of a text and how they have been or may be approached by the various exegetical techniques which we have discussed in the earlier chapters of this book. For example, if it becomes clear that the text contains references to historical persons, places, or events with which the interpreter is unfamiliar, the exegete should recognize that such questions belong to the general category of historical criticism. Accordingly, one should proceed to the investigation of different issues and problems by consulting and using the reference books and tools useful for providing such information.

(3) Utilize the tools appropriate to a given exegetical technique. As we have noted earlier, some exegetical tools and reference books are especially useful in unfolding certain dimensions of a text while others are more appropriate for other dimensions. A critical edition of the Bible which supplies information for variant wordings may be especially useful for textual-critical questions but only of little value for broader literary questions. At this point, the exegete is required to know what tools are available, the types of information each will yield, and how they may be used in concert with each other. This is best gained by developing first-hand acquaintance with them.

(4) Correlate the questions and answers addressed to this point. After the first several readings of a passage, and after several sets of questions and issues have been isolated and addressed, the exegete gradually discovers how interlocking these are. Quite often, a literary question will be seen to be related integrally to a historical one, and the answer to both may ultimately hinge upon the answer to a more theological question. At this point, the exegete's task must become more sophisticated as the attempt is made to correlate various kinds of techniques and types of criticism. In fact, what often emerges is another, entirely new set of questions or a set of old questions now more refined and sharpened. These the interpreter addresses in much the same fashion as earlier, always attentive to the various dimensions of a text and the various kinds of tools useful to addressing them.

(5) Conclude the analysis. These initial levels of investigation may be viewed as analysis, in the stricter sense of "breaking down" the exegetical work into its component parts. Here the exegete's task is to "break down" the passage, examine its language, structure, and all its various components, with a view to seeing them both in isolation and in relation to each other. Sometimes, pursuing one exegetical procedure will lead to

another, but just as often, one will have to make a concerted effort to examine each part of the passage and to pursue various exegetical techniques, even if they seem to bear no clear relation to the other parts and procedures. The goal here is to make sure that one has tackled all those aspects of a passage which might conceivably be related to producing an overall interpretation. It often happens that the exegete spends much time in examining aspects of the passage which turn out, in the end, not to be very relevant to the final exegesis at all. Unfortunately, this is in the very nature of research and cannot easily be avoided.

(6) Synthesize the findings into a coherent interpretation of the passage. This usually turns out to be the most difficult stage of an exegesis, primarily because it requires selectivity. After the exegete has completed the formal stage of analyzing the passage, it now remains to survey the field, assess one's findings, and then decide how they may best be put together to produce an illuminating interpretation of the passage. This often means that the material will be presented in the exegesis paper itself in an order totally out of sequence from that of the investigation. For example, one might have engaged in historical criticism at the very end of one's analysis, and the nature of the text may have required this. Yet, upon reflection, the exegete may decide that it is precisely this aspect of the passage which will need to be discussed first in an exegesis paper. Thus, the order in which the basic exegetical research was carried out may not necessarily be the order in which the final exegesis is unfolded.

This stage of synthesis requires the exegete to weigh each part of the investigation in light of other parts. In the analytical stage, a great amount of time might have been spent on answering certain questions, yet, on reflection, the exegete may decide that all of this research may be telescoped into a very short space.

Conversely, what might have required only a short amount of research time may actually require several paragraphs of elaboration in the exegesis itself. Here, it becomes a question of balance. The exegete must have developed enough familiarity with the passage to be able to decide which aspects of the passage need full elaboration and which do not. No clear-cut answer to this aspect of synthesis can be given in the abstract.

Another important consideration at this stage of preparing an exegesis is to allow sufficient time for the synthesis to occur. A common mistake made by beginning students is failing to allow enough time for the information gained in the analysis stage to jell. In fact, one of the reasons that exegesis papers often turn out to be a potpourri of miscellaneous facts and observations is that the analysis stage was hurried and not enough time was allowed for the interpreter to sift out the less important details in order to discern those aspects of the passage which truly require illumination and elaboration. This is best remedied, first of all, by establishing a definite point of terminating the analysis stage. The exegete will soon discover that the analytical stage is, in one sense, interminable, for there may be literally no limit to how far one can investigate a passage. Yet, realistically the analytical research must be concluded, and it can be, as long as one has established appropriate time limitations and provided one has focused on centrally important questions.

Second, once the exegetical analysis has been concluded, it is quite often most helpful to let the material set for a while. This will often allow the exegetical dust to settle long enough to enable the exegete to see the overall terrain from a better perspective. Moreover, this jelling period will often allow time for certain parts to fit into a larger scheme, and the synthesis, in this case, will have already occurred to a large degree before the final writing of the exegesis paper actually begins. Obviously, as in every writing project, certain things will not become fully clear until one begins writing, but much will have become clear, and the more synthesis one can achieve before the final writing, the better.

CHAPTER 12

Employing the Fruits of
BIBLICAL EXEGESIS

The Bible is read, used, and interpreted in many different contexts and in many different ways in contemporary culture. The manifold ways in which the Bible is read and studied range from individual reading for general knowledge to college and university literature courses. In the former, it may be treated as one of the classical documents about which the educated person should be informed. In the latter, it may be treated as any other document from classical antiquity or explored for its literary and other influences on modern culture.

Within Judaism and Christianity, the Bible, of course, has the status of sacred text. Within these two religious communities, the Bible, as Scripture, has been ascribed and plays a normative role. As such, it is read and employed in special ways, in ways that are different from those of the general reading public or of the student in a comparative literature course. Within these communities of faith, the Bible has various functions.

Both Jews and Christians use the Scriptures to reconstruct the early history of their communities. Both communities use the Bible as a resource for understanding and formulating their beliefs and theologies. Both use the Scriptures within the context of public worship where they are read and used for preaching and proclamation. Both Jews and Christians utilize the Bible for personal appropriation and for insight and guidance in multiple aspects of life.

Exegesis is involved in all of these uses of the Bible, in its general and "non-religious" use as well as in its specific employment within the life of religious communities. How exegesis is done and the impact of exegesis on the use of the Bible is of special significance within the life of these religious communities. It is within these communities and the academic institutions associated with them that exegesis and biblical interpretation are most frequently a matter of concern and raised to the level of conscious discussion. It is within the life of these communities that exegetes function in their most significant roles.

Within the life of the church and synagogue, exegesis should be a conscious operation in all phases of the use of the Bible—in historical reconstruction, in the formation of theology, in preaching and proclamation, and in personal appropriation.

In this final chapter, we want to explore how the exegetical process is related to these aspects of the use of the Bible in the life of the church and synagogue and how the student can move from the performance of exegesis to the utilization of exegesis in the various disciplines of biblical usage.

For Historical and Archaeological Reconstruction

One of the results of post-Enlightenment investigations of Scripture was the change in perspective toward biblical texts and their utilization for historical reconstruction. Prior to this time, the story of Israel and the early church as it was unfolded in the narratives of the Bible and in the traditional interpretation of these narratives was regarded as historical. How the Bible presented this story was assumed to be the "way it happened." The narratives were read so that the course of events was identified with the story line of the texts.

This unqualified identification of the biblical story with the history of Israel and the early church came to be modified for several reasons. The rise of modern science posed a serious challenge to biblical chronology. It became clear that the earth was more than the six thousand years old which a strict adherence to biblical chronology suggested. Historical and documentary criticisms made clear that the Bible unfolds not one but several "stories of Israel." Analysis of the literature uncovered various sources or accounts within the Pentateuch and the historical books, each of these presenting a different point of view. The narrative literature was seen as motivated primarily by religious and theological interests rather than purely historiographical concerns. That is, they were seen to be advocating particular perspectives or viewpoints on the history as much as reporting history.

Similar changes occurred with respect to the New Testament. For centuries it had been assumed, more or less uncritically, that the story of the life of Jesus and the early church as unfolded in the four Gospels and the Acts of the Apostles was the way it happened; the biblical story was also biblical history, it was thought. What was assumed to be needed for the Gospels was a harmonization of their accounts. Gradually it dawned on biblical interpreters that the Gospels are more theological than historical in nature. Acts also was acknowledged as a theological writing. Scholars recognized that far from presenting a comprehensive account of the early church, it actually only presented an account of its growth and development westward, from Jerusalem to Rome. Moreover, its choice of important characters was seen to be highly selective. Rather than being a comprehensive account of "the acts of the apostles," on closer inspection it was discovered to be actually an account of "some of the acts of some of the apostles," most notably Peter and Paul.

The radical impact on biblical studies of the post-Enlightenment period can be seen in the way it forced interpreters to take history and historical perspectives seriously: the Bible is a product of a historical process and therefore has its rootage in human culture; the Bible is a book anchored in the past and is therefore distanced in thought and outlook from the present; and the Bible is an anthology of ancient writings and therefore should be subjected to the same critical analysis as all other such writings.

Today historians of Israelite and early church history, like their "secular" counterparts, take certain stances toward the Bible and the reconstruction of history that differ considerably from their earlier counterparts. First of all, this involves a more critical stance toward the sources. These are no longer taken as purely factual reporting but as documents influenced by various theological and sociological concerns, different historical contexts, and different purposes and intentions. Thus a biblical text or narrative must be thoroughly exegeted and evaluated as to how it can be used for historical reconstruction. The exegesis of reports about what happened and the reconstruction of what might have happened are thus closely related but are by no means identical. Second, attempts are made to reconstruct the history without appeal either to special divine intervention in history or miraculous occurrences which might have altered the course of events. This represents a rather radical break with the outlook of the sources themselves which speak of divine involvement in historical events. The modern historian tends to consider this theological dimension in the texts to be a reflection of the faith and theology of the communities and the authors rather than a datum of history itself which can be studied and confirmed. Third, historians are aware that they are not writing a definitive history—"the history"—and narrating once and for all the ways things actually happened. Historians recognize that they are children of their age with biases and limited knowledge and perspectives and that "history" is a reconstruction of the past based on the knowledge and experiences of the present—often informed by a lot of intuition.

Just as historians no longer write the history of Israel and the early church by retelling the biblical story, neither are they any longer bound just to the evidence of the Bible. In recent years, the discipline of archaeology has entered the picture. Archaeological excavations and remains, especially in the last century, have become available which can be utilized for reconstructing historical events and conditions. Some of these remains are written sources—inscriptions and other texts—but most are non-written artifacts. Texts can usually be dated, on the basis of contents, language, and mode of writing, to general historical periods and often offer specific historical information. Other artifacts, such as pottery, architectural remains, skeletons, and jewelry, provide general types of knowledge—information about people's styles of life, levels of culture, means of livelihood, and types of habitation. All of the unwritten archaeological evidence comes out of the ground uninterpreted. The archaeologists and historians must interpret the data, generally in light of other evidence and particularly the written sources, especially the Bible. Contrary to much popular opinion the purpose of archaeology per se is neither to prove nor disprove the Bible. Archaeology is by nature a neutral discipline. While archaeology can illumine the actual course of Israelite and early Christian history, it can neither prove nor disprove the theological and faith claims of the biblical record.

In using a biblical text to reconstruct a part of the history and archaeology of ancient Israel and the early church, that is, in moving from exegesis to historical reconstruction, the biblical student must keep several factors in mind.

(1) Exegesis of the material is a prerequisite. Exegesis will allow the interpreter to answer such questions as: To what genre of literature does the text belong? What type of historical information can one expect to gain from such a genre? To what source or sources does the text belong? What are the tendencies and theological concerns of this source which may have influenced the particular presentation in the text? From what historical period does the text or source come and how

might this context have influenced the text? What cultural and socio-logical knowledge might be gained from the text? If the text does not provide explicit and intentional historical evidence, does it provide any implicit or unintentional evidence that can be used for historical reconstruction?

(2) Other texts relevant to the same event or time must be exegeted and correlated with the primary text. Often different presentations of the same episode will be found. This is the case, for example, with many narratives, such as those about the conquest of Canaan (Joshua 1—12 compared with Judges 1) and some events in the reign of Jehoshaphat (1 Kings 22:48–49 compared with 2 Chronicles 20:35–37). After these parallel texts have been exegeted, they must be compared, differences noticed and appraised, and historical probability assessed.

(3) Non-biblical source material which might relate to the issue under consideration should be brought into consideration. Even such non-biblical material must be submitted to exegesis with similar procedures applied as those used in biblical exegesis.

(4) Relevant archaeological data should be drawn upon where this exists or its absence noted where this is the case. Where archaeological evidence exists, it can generally be utilized to supplement the textual evidence. To take a specific example, this would be the case with such evidence as material from Hazor, Megiddo, and Gezer from the time of Solomon if one were working on the passage in 1 Kings 9:15–16. In other cases, archaeological evidence raises questions about the historical reliability of a biblical report. For example, Joshua 7:1—8:29 reports on the Israelite capture of a large, fortified city at Ai. Excavations at the site of ancient Ai (*et-tell* in modern Palestine) have shown that the site was unoccupied from about 2000 to 1150 B.C. and that after reoccupation, the site was actually a small village not a major city. Here we have a case where archaeological evidence calls into question the historicity of a biblical account and requires a reassessment of how one reads and uses the biblical account.

The reconstruction of an event in biblical history must, therefore, be the consequence of correlating various forms of evidence drawn from biblical and non-biblical literary evidence and from non-literary archaeological evidence. The importance of each of these aspects must be evaluated in each particular case. At the very heart of reconstruction, however, is exegesis. Since the Bible is the primary, and at times the only, source for reconstructing biblical history, this only emphasizes the indispensability of the exegetical process.

For Doing Theology

The task of theology, as a specialized discipline, is to articulate the faith of the synagogue and the church for each new generation of believers. Professional theologians, both academic and ministerial, do this on a sustained, regular basis. Active and intentional theological reflection, however, is not the exclusive prerogative of professional theologians. Nonprofessional or lay theologians engage in the same type of activity. In fact, anyone who makes a conscious, concerted effort to reflect on one's faith and give organized shape to these reflections is engaged in doing theology.

A dynamic way of viewing the theological task is to see it as giving shape to all of those aspects and dimensions of faith which figure in the explicit formulation of belief. The theologian becomes responsible for the whole of reality, and for all fields of knowledge, and finds it necessary to bring these to bear on faith, both as a phenomenon in its own right and as a system of thought.

As theologians reflect upon the reality of faith, its multiple dimensions, and the settings in which it occurs, they find it necessary to organize and arrange these more systematic and theoretical reflections into meaningful patterns for the benefit of the believing communities. The theologian works from a bifocal vantage point which seeks to do full justice both to the experiential dimension of faith, the "lived lives" of the believing communities, as well as to the more intellectual, theoretical, or cognitive dimension of faith as it comes to be formulated in discursive language. Consequently, the theologian is both informed by as well as informs the community of believers whose faith is being systematized and articulated.

Theologians seek to articulate the faith of each generation not only by relating it to previous formulations of the past but also by formulating it in terms drawn from the present. The faith thus finds itself responsible to history but also responsible to the present as it attempts to explain the faith to the modern world in light of modern thought and knowledge. For this reason, the work of theologians has to be redone in each generation.

Theology achieves its task by seeking to explicate the ways in which believers have thought about central theological realities, issues, and problems such as God or anthropology and also by suggesting appropriate ways for this to be done given the current status of intellectual thought. In this constructive task, theologians naturally regard the Bible as an indispensable source, not only because the Bible itself, in one sense, represents the earliest (Jewish and Christian) theological thought but also because the Bible still functions as normative in shaping faith and practice within modern communities of faith.

Because theologians operate with general categories and because the Bible constitutes one source for doing theology, along with philosophy, science, humanistic studies, as well as other fields of knowledge, the way in which theologians use the Bible is functionally different from the way in which a historian, a minister, or the ordinary person uses it. In attempting to construct an imaginative theological statement about God, the theologian will naturally consult, appeal to, and adduce those parts of Scripture or biblical formulations and concepts which bear most directly on this topic. At an earlier period, constructing systematic theologies was achieved in a type of proof-texting fashion, where all the passages pertaining to or assumed to be supportive of a particular doctrine were collected and arranged in some ordered fashion. In the light of modern biblical criticism, theologians now recognize this to be an improper use of Scripture. Consequently, in their constructive theological work, they too take into account the historical dimension of the biblical texts. Not every text concerned with a particular topic will be seen to have equal value merely because it appears in the Bible. Theologians are also heavily indebted to critical exegesis for its assistance in uncovering the various theological perspectives within the Bible. Although at one time it was more or less assumed that the Bible, from start to finish, presented a single theological message, theologians now recognize the wide diversity or plurality of theological perspectives within Scripture and take this into account in their theological work.

For the beginning exegete, the work of theologians can be valuable in several ways. Because of their long-standing commitment to Scripture as a central source in doing theology, they too engage in exegesis and are dependent upon the results of exegetical work. The form in which their exegetical results are presented naturally differs from that of biblical exegetes whose work most often takes the form of commentaries or books and articles on specific passages of Scripture.

Because theologians have examined biblical texts systematically by proceeding from broad and general universal categories and because they have examined a wide variety of texts as they relate to a specific topic or category, their angle of vision can be quite useful to the beginning exegete. In working on a passage, the exegete may discover that it makes significant claims pertaining to the nature or work of God. At this point, consulting those sections of both biblical and systematic theologies devoted to the doctrine of God will often introduce the beginning exegete not only to rich discussions of the passage being exegeted but also to similar treatments of other related biblical passages. Because the form of commentaries or more specialized monographs normally does not permit this scope of treatment, comprehensive biblical and systematic theologies provide a major resource of insights for the biblical exegete.

Not only should the exegete consult the work of theologians but also the exegete who investigates biblical texts also becomes engaged in doing theology. Any attempt to study a biblical text, to understand it in its setting and relate it to other portions of the Bible which bear directly on it, often engages the exegete at a profound level. The exegete not only seeks to understand the issues presented by a text but also to engage those issues and to allow this intellectual engagement both to inform, sharpen, and challenge one's own understanding of reality. At this stage, the exegete who makes the move to more generalized perspectives is making the same move as the biblical or systematic theologian. When one allows the text to inform and call into question one's own self-understanding and one's understanding of the world, theology is being done.

What is important for the beginning exegete to realize is that in moving from doing exegesis to doing theology certain conceptual shifts are made. There is clearly a broadening of focus when one moves from a specific text to a broader range of texts. Yet, just as often, the movement is reciprocal, because as the exegete consults a broader range of texts and then returns to a particular text, a deeper understanding is brought to the exegetical process. In making these moves, the beginning exegete does well to remember that the autonomy of the text and its message must be respected. If one discovers the message of the text being exegeted to be in serious tension with previously conceived theological positions or reconstructions, rather than resolving the tension too easily or too quickly, the exegete may be called on to reexamine and even radically modify previously held theological convictions. By the same token, one may discover that exegesis of a text tends to reinforce previously held theological convictions. By recognizing that such tensions are present even within the biblical texts themselves, the exegete may not feel as compelled to resolve them as might be the case otherwise. Familiarity with the history of exegesis may introduce the interpreter to various possible resolutions and thus provide a series of hermeneutical options for interpreting the text itself.

The exegete who also engages in doing theology should remain responsible to the canons and norms of biblical exegesis. Indeed, in doing exegesis one will discover how pervasively exegetical the theological enterprise is and how theological the exegetical enterprise is. Where sacred texts exist, exegesis is required and remains indispensable to all systematic attempts to relate the message of a specific biblical text to the broader theological message and the formulation of belief.

For Proclamation

Employing the Bible in preaching presupposes that the biblical text is a central ingredient and for this reason exegesis is a fundamental prerequisite. Yet it is just as important to remember that exegesis and proclamation are distinct activities. The transition from text to sermon is a natural transition, but it is a transition nevertheless. It is as much of a mistake to assume that proclamation consists of doing exegesis as it is to assume that exegesis is essentially a form of preaching. Both exegesis and preaching may inform each other, but they should not be merged into a single, undifferentiated activity.

Using the Bible for the purpose of proclamation constitutes a distinctive function and presupposes a clearly defined "life setting." What distinguishes this use of the Bible from the one previously discussed, that of doing theology, may be said to be its occasional nature, as much as anything else. Both the professional theologian and the preacher have as their task the articulation of the faith in a modern setting. They both seek to bring to bear the whole of reality on the biblical text as they seek to interpret it, but they also seek to appropriate the text for a modern setting as it too is informed and shaped by the whole body of knowledge. Here we see that the minister, too, is theologian, albeit in a qualified sense. Both obviously are professionals in that both have clearly defined vocations and both take seriously the canonical status of the Scripture and its revelatory value.

The minister's task differs from the academic theologian's task in at least two ways. First, the situation which the minister addresses in the act of proclamation is more concrete and more specific and for this reason the act of proclamation is more occasional. When the Word of God is brought to bear at a given moment for a people congregated for the express purpose of "hearing the Word of God," something momentary and unrepeatable happens. No attempt is being made to state in a broad, generalized sense the meaning of faith for the contemporary setting.

Preaching is rather quite specific in its focus, and there is the awareness that once the congregation disperses, the moment of proclamation is over. The sermon may be preserved in the form of a written manuscript or tape recording but the initial act of proclamation cannot be recovered. This occasional dimension of proclamation is distinctive.

Also distinctive, as compared with the task of doing theology, is the nature of the audience. The intended audience of the theologian is normally the church at large, while the intended audience of the preacher is a visible, local congregation. The respective "life settings" are distinguishable in both size and location.

The exegetical task in these respectively different "life settings" is similar in some respects, different in others. The preacher, like the professional theologian, stands at the end of a long process of interpretation, and is responsible for recognizing the multiple dimensions of the biblical text, such as its historical and literary dimensions. Similarly, the preacher does well to acknowledge the diversity of theological outlook reflected within the biblical writings.

Because the homiletical task is so often directly anchored in a biblical text, whether in the form of a lectionary where the texts have been chosen in advance, or whether the choice of text is made by the individual preacher, proclamation often bears a more genetic relationship to exegesis than does theology. Especially is this the case with expository preaching, where the intention is to expound a biblical text or to invite the audience to enter and share the world of the text.

Whether a sermon is explicitly expository in that it seeks to unfold a biblical text for a congregation, or whether it is only implicitly expository in that it alludes to biblical texts or images in the course of making a broader point, the preacher nevertheless should be responsible to the canons of biblical exegesis. In fact, it might be said that biblical exegesis is as essential to the preacher's task as the Bible is to the preacher's sermon. If the sermon is pervasively biblical, the preacher's task is preeminently exegetical. If the sermon is only occasionally biblical, the preacher is no less obligated to practice responsible exegesis than is otherwise the case.

Moving from an exegesis to a sermon is not a simple matter. In fact, the process has two foci: the text with its ancient context and the sermon with its modern context. The tasks and problems involved in this move may be stated in three questions: How does one translate the form and content of the original text into another form and content? How does one assess both the ancient and modern contexts in order to see analogies and patterns of relationships? How can one be responsible to both the text and its context or the sermon and its context?

One way of beginning to grapple with the movement from text to sermon is to explore the way in which a text or tradition may have functioned in its original context or within the life of Israel and the early church. Broadly speaking, a text and its message can function in at least three ways: constitutively, prophetically, or advisorily. These three functions may be related to the three basic forms of ministry: priest, prophet, and sage (or teacher). This division is, of course, somewhat artificial and is offered merely as a lens through which to view the various ways a text can be used. Just as the various functions of ministry overlap and were and are frequently embodied in the same person or in a single act of ministry, so also a single text or tradition may function in more than one fashion depending on the manner and context of its usage.

To speak of a constitutive or priestly function of a text refers to its use in a supportive, enhancing, and celebrative fashion. Priestly or constitutive functions deal with human existence in terms of the reenactment of past experiences and traditions, normal sacred practice, and routine conditions. Festivals and rituals give expression to this mode of ministry which is oriented to the stabilization and encouragement of the community and individual and the appropriation of the past with its structures and words of salvation and redemption. In such, identity and self-understanding are not really called into question. This does not mean that judgment is not an aspect of the priestly function and usage since the traditions and rituals embody the ideal and thus function as a means of assessing present realities.

The prophetic function and text challenges the present, its commitments and orientation, and calls for new and sometimes radical revision and alteration. The prophetic perspective critically views the present and the contemporary in terms of new viewpoints and different orientations. These perspectives challenge and sometimes threaten the identity, self-understanding, and customary behavior of the community. The prophetic may issue its challenge by drawing upon the traditions and views of the past or by appeal to the future. It may be a word of judgment and conviction or a word of hope and persuasion. It may announce death or life, but it is a word strongly evaluative of present conditions. It seeks not to constitute but to reconstitute.

The advisory function—the function of the sage or the wise—has as its goal the offering of instruction, wisdom, or insight without the overt desire either to confirm the present and its conditions or to call for reconstitution or reformation. It makes its appeal on the basis of general experience and seeks to illuminate rather than create conditions. Such illumination, however, may itself be catalytic and open up new perspectives which can lead to reconstitution.

The exegete in moving from an exegesis of the text to a sermon on the text should keep in mind both the original function of the text and the perceived function of the sermon. The function of the sermon within its context should not do damage to or be irresponsible to the original function and meaning of the text. The exegete as minister will, of course, have to assess the present needs and conditions of the audience as well as the intent of the preaching occasion and determine whether the sermon should function constitutively, prophetically, or advisorily. When bringing the message of the ancient text to bear on the modern situation, the role of analogy is important. The preacher should ask such questions as the following: What situation in the contemporary world and the immediate congregation is analogous to the situation addressed in the text? How are the participants in the modern situation analogous to those—the speaker, the audience, ancient Israel, the early church—in the original situation? What form and content should be given in and to the sermon in order for it to serve an analogous function in the modern situation as the text in its situation? How can the total context of ''what it meant'' inform and enlighten ''what it means''?

Preaching from the Bible and attempting to remain responsible to the text do not mean that the minister cannot orchestrate the text differently, by calling forth and emphasizing dimensions of the text that are actually recessive rather than dominant within the text. The minister may choose to tone down or modify dominant themes within the text. Here, the minister's role is not unlike that of the orchestra conductor who interprets a musical score. By respecting the autonomy of the text, the conductor may leave the score completely intact, making no attempt to change the original composer's musical message, yet after having thoroughly examined and studied the score, the conductor may feel free to interpret the piece for a particular occasion. This form of orchestration does no injustice to the composer's intentions. It is rather the conductor's responsibility to interpret the text for modern listeners.

Similarly, the minister's task is to read and to understand, and also to interpret the text for the modern congregation of believers. This may mean that the minister's sermon ''orchestrates'' the text variously from time to time, but this can be done without doing injustice to the text or without engaging in irresponsible exegesis.

The exegetical procedures, when they detect the multilayered quality of some texts, may in fact open up a text to multiple preaching possibilities. A parable of Jesus, for example, may be orchestrated in preaching according to a diversity of "original" contexts—in the ministry of Jesus, in the oral tradition of the church, and in its diverse usage in Matthew, Mark, and Luke.

Finally, the exegete-preacher must be warned that the one who engages in thorough exegesis may often discover that certain interpretations of texts, even cherished ones, are not viable, and cannot be incorporated into a sermon. Here, the negative function of exegesis is at work, placing limitations on the minister, even as it does in other ways on the historian or theologian.

For Personal Appropriation

Just as the Bible is the possession of historians, theologians, and preachers, so is it the possession of all who read it for moral guidance, spiritual edification, or even pleasure. The person who reads the Bible for these purposes may not be motivated by professional interests, but this does not mean that exegesis is any less absent or necessary. If exegesis is the process through which one comes to an informed understanding of a biblical text, it becomes as essential for the nonprofessional reader as it is for the professional reader. For that matter, the professional reader who reads the Bible for personal appropriation does not cease to do exegesis when such a shift in purpose occurs. That one does exegesis does not change, although why one does exegesis may change.

Rather than viewing the work of biblical scholars and other professional theologians and historians as preliminary or as that which can be laid aside when one reads the Bible for personal profit, the everyday reader can see oneself as part of a larger circle of interested readers and interpreters who, in the end, have a common interest. Those who have devoted full-time study to the Bible have most often done so in order to render service to those who cannot. When scholars are seen as working in the service of communities of faith, even if their work and the results of their research may appear to the layperson to be inimical to the faith and their efforts not always applauded, they should at least be taken seriously as one seeks to read and understand the Bible.

When the Bible is read for moral and spiritual guidance, the reader may be said to assume the position of "hearer," analogous to that of the original hearers to whom the writing was addressed. It will never be possible to escape the "third party" perspective discussed earlier, for subsequent readers of the Bible will always be those who overhear, rather than those who hear directly. Yet, the biblical writings have become canonized precisely because of their demonstrated capacity to transcend the immediate situation which they addressed, and historically they have done so. Regardless of their time-conditioned quality, they nevertheless possess an immediacy and the capability to address hearers and readers of subsequent ages quite directly. What distinguishes the one who reads the Bible for moral and spiritual guidance from the one who reads it in the service of history, theology, or preaching is the immediacy of the relationship between text and reader. Behind this stance is the assumption that the text is speaking or can speak directly to the needs of the reader.

This need not mean that one should read the Bible any less rigorously, certainly not any less critically, for the purposes of personal appropriation. Under no circumstances should one suspend critical judgment in reading the biblical text. Reading the Bible for moral and spiritual guidance also requires the reader to interrogate the text, and to do so rigorously, but the set of questions one brings to such a reading may differ vastly from those the historian brings to the text. One does well to remember that many of the procedures of biblical interpretation developed in response to questions which had arisen in the context of reading the Bible for personal and spiritual guidance. In fact, most, if not all, of the types of criticism discussed in the earlier chapters have been developed and refined as a means of making this type of Bible reading more, not less, understandable. Reading of the Bible for personal appropriation should be as attentive to the various dimensions of the text which these various techniques address as reading the Bible for professional reasons.

One way of articulating the stance or perspective of those who read the Bible for personal and spiritual guidance is to recognize that they "look along" the text more than "look at" the text. The former stance suggests the picture of one who is inside the text, standing within the tradition as it were, adopting the perspectives and outlooks suggested in the text, or at least, doing so provisionally. On reflection upon such reading, one may decide to adopt the posture and paradigms of the text, adapt them, or even reject them as unacceptable, but there is at least the initial willingness to place oneself within the range of the voice of the text and be willing both to hear and see. The latter stance—"looking at"—suggests the picture of one standing outside the text, "looking in," as it were. This need not imply a negative stance, nor even a detached, disinterested relationship to the text, but it is correct to say that the historian and theologian, as well as the preacher, are all using the text for some other purpose. For them, the biblical text has an indirect rather than a direct function, whereas for the one who reads the Bible for personal and spiritual edification, the text is often being read for its own sake. It is not unlike the difference between one who reads Shakespeare as a literary critic and one who does so for pleasure, for sheer intellectual stimulation, or for moral edification. While the latter sorts of concerns may originally have motivated the literary critic, and while they may continue to occur even as the literary critic carries out his or her professional work, the work of literary criticism, by its very nature, requires the reader to "look at" the text in a way that is functionally different from "looking along" the text.

Reading the Bible for personal appropriation should not be conceived in a narrowly personalistic sense as if the person's own spiritual or moral needs are always the primary end in view. Even the use of the Bible by artists should be included here. When the Bible is read and appropriated through artistic creativity, whether it is in the form of music, painting, drama, or any of the other forms of artistic expression, exegesis is also carried out, even if it appears to be implicit. Handel's *Messiah* presupposes an exegesis of various portions of the Bible, as does MacLeish's *JB*, and in both cases the biblical text has been read and exegeted prior to the artistic production which has resulted from such interpretation. Indeed, these resulting interpretations are not essentially different from other forms of interpretation, including historical, theological, homiletical, or ethical interpretations. They differ only in form, not in essence. Professional exegetes may also learn much from these artistic appropriations of the Bible and biblical themes.

The beginning exegete should be alert to the various ways within modern culture in which the biblical text is appropriated and should by now realize that exegesis is common to all of them. One might well ask whether Zeffirelli's film, *The Gospel According to St. Matthew*, is best understood as a form of historical reconstruction or artistic appropriation, or even as a kind of theological reconstruction if not biblical proclamation. It may turn out to be some of each, but this should come as no surprise, for we have seen that even the historian who deals with the biblical texts, at certain junctures, must also deal with literary, theological, homiletical, moral, and artistic dimensions of the texts. Modern readers of the Bible often find themselves sensitive to the many dimensions of the biblical text. The beginning exegete who wishes to read the Bible with an informed understanding can do no less.

BIBLIOGRAPHY

Exegesis and Historical-Archaeological Reconstruction

Abraham, W. J., *Divine Revelation and the Limits of Historical Criticism* (London/New York: Oxford University Press, 1982).

Albright, W. F., "Archaeology Confronts Biblical Criticism" in *American Scholar* 7 (1938) 176–88.

Barr, J., "Story and History in Biblical Theology" in *Journal of Religion* 56 (1976) 1–17.

Dahl, N. A., "The Problem of the Historical Jesus" in his *The Crucified Messiah and Other Essays* (Minneapolis: Augsburg Publishing House, 1974) 48–89.

*Dever, W. G., *Archaeology and Biblical Studies: Retrospects and Prospects* (Evanston: Seabury-Western, 1974).

Dever, W. G., "Archaeology" in *Interpreter's Dictionary of the Bible, Supplementary Volume*, 44–52.

Dever, W. G., "Biblical Theology and Biblical Archaeology" in *Harvard Theological Review* 73 (1980) 1–15.

*Finkelstein, J. J., "The Bible, Archaeology, and History: Have the Excavations Corroborated Scripture?" in *Commentary* 28 (1959) 341–49.

*Harvey, V. A., *The Historian and the Believer* (New York/London: Macmillan Company/SCM Press, 1966/1967; reissued, Philadelphia: Westminster Press, 1981).

Jeremias, J., *The Problem of the Historical Jesus* (rev. ed.; Philadelphia: Fortress Press, 1971).

Lapp, P. W., *Archaeology and History* (New York: World Publishing Company, 1969).

McArthur, H. K., *The Quest Through the Centuries: The Search for the Historical Jesus* (Philadelphia: Fortress Press, 1966).

McArthur, H. K., *In Search of the Historical Jesus* (New York/London: Charles Scribner's Sons/SPCK, 1969/1970).

*Miller, J. M., *The Old Testament and the Historian* (Philadelphia/London: Fortress Press/SPCK, 1976).

Sasson, J. M., "On Choosing Models for Recreating Israelite Pre-Monarchic History" in *Journal for the Study of the Old Testament* 21 (1981) 3–24.

Schweitzer, A., *The Quest of the Historical Jesus: A Critical Study of Its Progress from Reimarus to Wrede* (London/New York: A. & C. Black/Macmillan Company, 1910/1950).

Wright, G. E., "What Archaeology Can and Cannot Do" in *Biblical Archaeologist* 34 (1971) 70–76.

de Vaux, R., "On Right and Wrong Uses of Archaeology" in *Near Eastern Archaeology in the Twentieth Century* (ed. by J. A. Sanders; Garden City: Doubleday & Company, 1970) 64–80.

Exegesis and Doing Theology

Achtemeier, P. J., *An Introduction to the New Hermeneutic* (Philadelphia: West-minster Press, 1969).

Barr, J., "Biblical Theology" in *Interpreter's Dictionary of the Bible, Supplementary Volume*, 104–11.

Barth, K., *Church Dogmatics* (Edinburgh/New York: T. & T. Clark/Charles Scribner's Sons, 1936 1/1. 98–212.

Bartlett, D. L., *The Shape of Scriptural Authority* (Philadelphia: Fortress Press, 1983).

Childs, B. S., *Biblical Theology in Crisis* (Philadelphia: Westminster Press, 1970).

Ebeling, G., "The Meaning of Biblical Theology" in his *Word and Faith* (Philadelphia/London: Fortress Press/SCM Press, 1963) 79–97.

Frei, H. W., *Eclipse of Biblical Narrative: A Study in Eighteenth and Nineteenth Century Hemeneutics* (New Haven/London: Yale University Press, 1974).

Hanson, P. D., *The Diversity of Scripture: A Theological Interpretation* (Philadelphia: Fortress Press, 1982).

Johnston, R. K. (ed.), *The Use of the Bible in Theology: Evangelical Options* (Atlanta: John Knox Press, 1985).

Kaufman, G. D., "What Shall We Do with the Bible?" in *Interpretation* 25 (1971) 95–112.

*Kehm, G., "Scripture and Tradition" in *Christian Theology: An Introduction to Its Tradition and Tasks* (ed. by P. C. Hodgson and R. H. King; Philadelphia: Fortress Press, 1982).

*Kelsey, D. H., *The Uses of Scripture in Recent Theology* (Philadelphia/London: Fortress Press/SCM Press, 1975/1976).

*Kelsey, D. H., "The Bible and Christian Theology " in *Journal of the American Academy of Religion* 48 (1980) 385–402.

McKim, D. K., *What Christians Believe About the Bible* (Nashville: Thomas Nelson, 1985).

McKim, D. K. (ed.), *A Guide to Contemporary Hermeneutics: Major Trends in Biblical Interpretation* (Grand Rapids: Eerdmans Publishing Company, 1986).

Nineham, D., *The Use and Abuse of the Bible* (London/New York: Macmillan Press Ltd./Barnes and Noble, 1976).

Pannenberg, W., "The Crisis of the Scripture Principle" in his *Basic Questions in Theology: Collected Essays* (Philadelphia/London: Fortress Press/SCM Press, 1970) 1. 1–14.

Rahner, K., "Exegesis and Dogmatic Theology" in his *Theological Investigations* (New York/London: Seabury Press/Darton, Longman and Todd, 1966) 5. 67–93.

Smart, J. D., *The Past, Present, and Future of Biblical Theology* (Philadelphia/Edinburgh: Westminster Press/T. & T. Clark, 1979/1980).

Stendahl, K., "Biblical Theology, Contemporary" in *Interpreter's Dictionary of the Bible*, 1. 418–32.

*Stroup, G., "Revelation" in *Christian Theology: An Introduction to Its Tradi-

tions and Tasks (ed. by P. C. Hodgson and R. H. King; Philadelphia: Fortress Press, 1982).

Wainwright, A., *Beyond Biblical Criticism: Encountering Jesus in Scripture* (Atlanta/London: John Knox Press/SPCK, 1982).

Exegesis and Proclamation

Achtemeier, E., *The Old Testament and the Proclamation of the Gospel* (Philadelphia: Westminster Press, 1973).

Barclay, W., *Communicating the Gospel* (Edinburgh: St. Andrews Press, 1978).

*Barrett, C. K., *Biblical Preaching and Biblical Scholarship* (London: Epworth Press, 1957) = *Biblical Problems and Biblical Preaching* (Philadelphia: Fortress Press, 1964) 28–49.

*Best, E., *From Text to Sermon: Responsible Use of the New Testament in Preaching* (Atlanta/Edinburgh: John Knox Press/St. Andrews Press, 1978).

Brown, R. E., "Hermeneutics" in *The Jerome Biblical Commentary* (ed. by R. E. Brown et al.; Englewood Cliffs/London: Prentice-Hall/Geoffrey Chapman, 1968) 2. 605–23.

Cox, J. W., *A Guide to Biblical Preaching* (Nashville: Abingdon Press, 1976).

Craddock, F. B., *Overhearing the Gospel: Preaching and Teaching the Faith to Persons Who Have Already Heard* (Nashville: Abingdon Press, 1978).

Craddock, F. B., *As One Without Authority* (3d ed.; Nashville: Abingdon Press, 1979).

Craddock, F. B., "Occasion—Text—Sermon" in *Interpretation 35* (1981) 59–71.

*Craddock, F. B., *Preaching* (Nashville: Abingdon Press, 1985) 99–150.

Fuller, R. H., *The Use of the Bible in Preaching* (Philadelphia/London: Fortress Press/Bible Reading Fellowship, 1981).

Gowan, D. E., *Reclaiming the Old Testament for the Christian Pulpit* (Atlanta/Edinburgh: John Knox Press/T. & T. Clark, 1980/1981).

Keck, L. E., *The Bible in the Pulpit: The Renewal of Biblical Preaching* (Nashville: Abingdon Press, 1978).

Keck, L. E., "Listening To and Listening For: From Text to Sermon (Acts 1:8)" in *Interpretation 27* (1973) 184–202.

Keck, L. E., *Taking the Bible Seriously* (Nashville: Abingdon Press, 1979).

Manson, T. W., "Preaching and Exegesis" in *Neutestamentliche Studien für Rudolf Bultmann* (ed. by W. Eltester; Berlin: Alfred Töpelmann, 1954) 10–14.

Mezger, M., "Preparation for Preaching—The Route from Exegesis to Proclamation" in *Journal for Theology and the Church* 2 (1965) 159–79.

Murphy, R. E. (ed.), *Theology, Exegesis, and Proclamation* (New York/Edinburgh: Herder and Herder/T. & T. Clark, 1971).

Sanders, J. A., "Hermeneutics" in *Interpreter's Dictionary of the Bible, Supplementary Volume*, 402–7.

Sanders, J. A., *God Has a Story Too: Sermons in Context* (Philadelphia: Fortress Press, 1979).

Smart, J. D., *The Strange Silence of the Bible in the Church: A Study in Hermeneutics* (Philadelphia/London: Westminster Press/SCM Press, 1970).

Smith, D. M., *Interpreting the Gospels for Preaching* (Philadelphia: Fortress Press, 1980).

Thiselton, A. C., *The Two Horizons: New Testament Hermeneutics and Philosophical Description* (Exeter/Grand Rapids: Paternoster Press/Eerdmans Publishing Company, 1979/1980).

Thompson, W. D., *Preaching Biblically: Exegesis and Interpretation* (Nashville: Abingdon Press, 1981).

Exegesis and Personal Appropriation

Barr, J., *The Bible in the Modern World* (London/New York: SCM Press/Harper & Row, 1977).

*Brueggemann, W., *The Creative Word: Canon as a Model for Biblical Education* (Philadelphia: Fortress Press, 1982).

Capps, D., *Biblical Approaches to Pastoral Counseling* (Philadelphia: Westminster Press, 1981).

Davidson, R., *The Bible in Religious Education* (Edinburgh/New York: Handsel Press/Columbia University Press, 1980).

*Gustafson, J. M., "The Place of Scripture in Christian Ethics: A Methodological Study" and "The Relation of the Gospels to the Moral Life" in his *Theology and Christian Ethics* (New York: Pilgrim Press, 1974) 121–59.

Gustafson, J. M., *Christ and the Moral Life* (Chicago/London: University of Chicago Press, 1979).

Holmer, P. L., *The Grammar of Faith* (San Francisco: Harper & Row, 1978).

Sleeper, C. F., "Ethics as a Context for Biblical Interpretation" in *Interpretation* 22 (1968) 443–60.

*Wink, W., *The Bible in Human Transformation: Towards a New Paradigm for Biblical Study* (Philadelphia: Fortress Press, 1973).

Wink, W., *Transforming Bible Study: A Leader's Guide* (Nashville/London: Abingdon Press/SCM Press, 1980).